I Didn't See You There:

The poetic memoirs of one family's journey through mental health crisis, diagnosis and embracing neurodivergence.

Foreword

Dear and Gentle Reader ;)
What an honour it was to be asked to write the foreword to "I Didn't See You There".

Charlotte and I first connected around 3 years ago. It was during the time that I was getting ready to republish Your Child Is Not Broken, my Sunday Times bestseller, about life as a parent of an autistic child who hit burnout and crashed out of school.

Charlotte and I chatted online and a friendship quickly blossomed. Our teenage children were of similar ages, we'd faced some of the same challenges in trying to unlock support for them, and we shared the same silly sense of humour. Many times I'd open a WhatsApp notification to find a hilarious, mildly-inappropriate, meme from Charlotte that would see me burst into fits of giggles. Her messages brought me much-needed moments of joy and release whilst I was editing the book and reliving the traumatic events of my son's battle with autistic burnout.

It was early 2022 when Charlotte started shared some of her poems with me. I remember it was after a particularly tricky weekend in both our homes and Charlotte's words gave me so much comfort. That moment, I knew her poetry had the power to give a voice to parents like me. Parents who felt like we were drowning. Parents living in survival mode.

Charlotte's friendship and the poems she shared with me brought me so much solace. Through her words, I felt seen, acknowledged, understood. So when I was given the opportunity to include one of her poems in Your Child Is Not Broken, I didn't hesitate. I chose The House of Cards, which is still one of my favourite pieces.

Charlotte's work has a beautiful simplicity about it at the same time as being deeply moving. Her words flood off the page and wrap you in a big warm hug which, when needed, you can collapse into and sob. And when you're done sobbing, you turn the page, read the next poem and let her words comfort you, stroke your head gently and tell you it's all going to be okay.

Often, as parents in Neurodivergent households, we become, by necessity, focussed solely on silent survival. In amplifying our children's voices and advocating for them in systems and situations where we must focus on what they need, we can lose our sense of self. Our needs, wants, wishes and desires are packed away in a box, marked "low priority" as we do what's needed to support our children. Charlotte's poetry speak to this. She doesn't shy away from the difficult conversations, thoughts, and emotions we might have. Reading her poetry has always felt to me like sitting at the kitchen table with a dear dear friend who understands me, without judgement. Who nods kindly and says "I've got you."

This collection of poems is a profound journey through the full spectrum of emotions experienced by SEND parents—hope, healing, and optimism intertwined with despair and sadness. Life is inherently full of contrasts, but for those of us raising children with special educational needs and disabilities, these contrasts often feel even sharper. What stands out most in this collection, however, is its potential to be a path toward healing. For those of us who have felt unheard, overlooked, or lost in the complexities of caregiving, these poems offer a voice, a sense of validation, and a reminder that we are not alone.

"I Didn't See You There" tackles head on - and without shame - the complex feelings experienced in households living under the shadow of mental health crisis, OCD, self harm and behaviour that challenges. But it's not a collection of despair: this is a collection about the ever-enduring power of love.

Charlotte's poems paint an honest picture of the life behind closed doors that some people will never experience or understand. She does so with such beautiful honesty that - rather than being soul crushingly depressing - this collection is a beacon of hope. Hope for recovery, hope for peace, hope for a time when we might start living again. Her poems are also a celebration of those mini victories: moments of connection, and the pure joy that comes with being a parent of a child who does live differently.

Just as Charlotte's poetry brought me solace and understanding whilst I was reliving the emotions and experiences of a very difficult time in my life, I feel sure that her words will do the same for other parents. My wish for you is that, through Charlotte's words, you find not just solace, but the strength to continue. I know that getting this book published has been a labour of love and challenge for Charlotte. I hope you will cherish it.

I also hope this collection brings you moments of light relief, just as Charlotte's meme of a painting of a "medieval woman with her emotional support dragon" did for me when I opened whatsapp this morning.

Sending much love from our House of Cards to yours,
Heidi

Heidi Mavir -Sunday Times Bestselling Author and Founder of EOTAS Matters

Testimonials

"Charlotte's work speaks to my lonely soul and soothes my tired heart. Her poems express what so many of us can't find the words for. This is poetry that validates, empowers and brings hope to those of us who have felt so alone for so long."
- Heidi Mavir, Best Selling Author of Your Child Is Not Broken, Founder of EOTAS Matters and Advocate.

"For me, the feelings are so clear and so brilliantly expressed with layers of nuance that resonate so much with those of us who deal with the challenges of neurodiversity either personally or via our loved ones. To hear parts of that journey written down by another and yet have it match your inner thoughts and feelings is breath-taking. And while at times it is the emotions of pain, sadness, struggle and exhaustion that we recognise, at others it is also the joy, awe, amazement and relief."
- Siobhan Adams, Headteacher

"Charlotte Gale, what a beautiful poem, powerful, poignant and so full of love!
Just wonderful. I think we need a whole book of these please! "
- Suzanne Alderson, Founder of Parenting Mental Health and Author of Never Let Go.

"Charlotte's poetry somehow precisely names and reveals the depths of pain and every other feeling that comes from being a parent to a mentally unwell child. She is able to lift the lid on something rarely spoken and reveal in stark clarity what parents of mentally unwell children are carrying inside. Touching, poignant and deeply moving. Much of her work brings me to tears and helps us all feel seen and just that bit less alone"

- Alisa

"Charlotte's poetry speaks to the community that she has found a place of belonging in; it inspires and gives truth to the many other families navigating neurodivergent diagnoses and helps us process our own feelings and experiences.

Charlotte has a raw talent that is not easily found and when she transcribes her emotions she takes us into a visceral world through her wonderful prose. Her use of personification to demystify and bring acceptance to mental illnesses is revolutionary and will open so many healthy discussions on this taboo.

As a parent (and a woman who has learnt to mask their neurodiversity) I have been able to embrace my own authenticity from living through Charlotte's beautiful memoirs."

- Danielle Jata-Hall, Author and Blogger, PDA Parenting

"These poems shine a light on situations that many families with neurodivergent children will experience. More than that, they give a window into the intense emotions that the battles with the system can often evoke in parents. They convey the pain and grief caused by others but also share positive aspects of the journey and of new beginnings. Full of emotion and very relatable."
- Steph, from Steph's Two Girls Blog

"While it's abundantly clear that Charlotte is naturally gifted with words, there is an unmistakable raw and understated quality to her poetry that speaks to the kind of wordplay that is only possible when the subject matter is experienced in the deepest, most honest way. I feel honoured to speak to her talent and authenticity and it fills me with hope knowing that her work will move, heal and impress upon others at a soul level."
- Dannii Bolton, Author, Please Don't At me- PDA Our Way.

"Having read 'Today I walked Among the Ghosts' I would have to say this is singularly the most beautiful thing that has ever fallen into my inbox.
Thank you so much. I'd like to wax lyrical about how amazing this is and how wonderful it made me feel but I don't want to sully your beautiful words by falling short in trying to emulate them. Simply beautiful" - Patch Hyde, The Fudge Patch, Greenwich

"Love, love, love this...so relatable, so true, so raw, so us"
- Sunny Dhillon

"Charlotte's work is testament to the fact, that experience is the key component when creating written art. Her ability to evoke emotion with her words, allows you, as a reader, to step into her shoes for a short while. And although my personal experience has very little overlap, it has opened doors in my mind. From heart-breaking honesty to exploding ecstasy, it is an honour to glance through a window into a different world"
- Daniel W, Teacher, Style Guru

Contents

Introduction

This is not what I imagined

OCD I hate you

Music stops, silence falls

The tale of the lonely lunchbox

There's always you

Anecdotes - Group 1

Mother's meltdown

The broken hangers

Stripped bare

From the kitchen floor

And so it begins

Outside the bathroom door

It's not about the ice cream

Anecdotes - Group 2

The shower

Blazer in a bin bag

The unthinkable

Lost

The birthday - part 1

The birthday - part 2

Footprints in the sand

Anecdotes - Group 3

The woman in the mirror

Acceptance

Steps

Making chilli

Ghosts

The moving staircase

Anecdotes - Group 4

In the dark

The glue

A beginning

Singing in the car

Friends with a twist

Anecdotes - Group 5

Listen to the professionals

Brainwashing

The faceless one

Happy Mother's Day

Through my eye

Monday morning

A glimpse of you

Dreams

Anecdotes - Group 6

The cancelled appointments

Meh

Chips by the river

Her hair

Christmas lights

Anecdotes - Group 7

Today she has left you

The place without boxes

Snapshot of a morning

Doing it your way

Anecdotes - Group 8

The phone

Self care

The cola bottle

The green flags

Cold coffee and car parks

Mother

Someone else's day

The kindness of strangers

Have you made the phone call?

To my future self

Anecdotes - Group 9

House of cards

Fishbowl families

Muffins and sunlight

The chair

Today they ate a cookie

The window

After the storm

My daughter of seasons

And I haven't made the crumble

Faded writing worn with time

There was a time

Just take a different route

The gap

I didn't see you there

Shepherds pie and scrambled eggs

Anecdotes - Group 10

Life in 3D

Oranges

Twilight Walk

Hope wrapped with a ribbon

Now you can see me

The calm before the storm

The beach

With laughter came light

Black magic

These are the boots

Authentically us

Down a long winding lane

The day she walked away

Afterward

Introduction

I'd like to start if I may with a confession.

I am sharing this incredibly personal anthology of poems and prose with you, under a pen name. I know that may make some of you feel I'm inauthentic or have unjustified delusions of grandeur. In fact nothing could be further from the truth.

Let me explain.

As our story unfolds there will be bleak darkness before light. I have authentically shared the raw reality of the last few years. It is, I feel, vital not to sugarcoat the truth if we are to break down the stigma of Mental illness and create genuine change and understanding. But, that is not the responsibility of my children. Therefore, for their autonomy of present and future choices- I am protecting their anonymity and that of my family.

I am writing as Charlotte, who found one day, quite by accident, that she'd actually written a book!

I never set out to write a book, you see.

I didn't.

One evening, a few years ago, I found myself sitting on my bed clenching my duvet so tightly that my knuckles wouldn't have looked out of place on a death defying rollercoaster. Because, that's what I was riding , metaphorically at least. Only there was no joy in the fear I felt.

Stomach churning terror, yes.

Rage, yes.

Hopelessness, yes.

Solitude, absolutely.

My youngest child, then 12, was mid an OCD meltdown. They were at that time teetering over the precipice of a full Mental Health Crisis and I, powerless to stop it, were to stand and watch. A spectator as this unchartered chapter unfolded.

Much of the support needed at that time, was a constant, reliable and neutral presence. A sounding board for their fury and fear. A safe space in which to be held. Sometimes in my arms, enveloped through the tears. And sometimes, like that night, from a small distance.

As I clutched my duvet, holding on for dear life, barely breathing under the weight of unshed tears, I reached for my phone. Not to call or text, not to doom scroll social media for distraction.

But to write.

As the words spilled onto the page that night, they carried with them the futility and pain so long locked inside.

And so
It began.

Writing our story (often from outside the bathroom door) whilst in the trenches of burnout, school based trauma and Mental illness became as necessary to me as food and water. Writing sustained me, it gave me hope that one day my words would reach others and in doing so bring comfort and light to those who found themselves living this strangely secular life, isolated from the rest of society, from family and friends, and feeling utterly lost.

As our world became small and volatile, I told our story.

I wrote of the pain, the messy, terrifying reality of hiding knives and removing locks from doors. Of keeping upstairs windows closed and voicing reasons to stay alive.

And, of another story ; that of a quieter, more subtle -but no less brutal- heartbreak.
A story, I now know to be true for so many, myself included.
A story of a girl who grew to be a young woman wrongly labelled as 'only anxious' and shackled by misconceptions and

societal stereotypes that robbed her of her neurodivergent identity.

A young woman who had to break, and with time and the right support, re-build the pieces so at last she could see and be seen.

This is a story of heartbreak. Of loss. Of enduring love, self discovery, diagnosis and finally of embracing authenticity.

It's messy and often dark. But, in stark contrast there are moments of humour. Of silliness and of laughter. Because that is the reality of living in a neuro-spicy household, with children who see through pretence, who see beauty in the mundane and soul in the smallest of lives. They are the spider Savers, the cloud watchers, the artists and dancers.
They are strong and fierce, despite the wounds and scars inflicted on them by outdated and broken systems.

They live among you, though often not seen.

They are the revolutionaries.

My children, and their neurokin.

I never set out to write a book;
Yet here it is.

And to my dearest daughter, I say once more,

I'm so very sorry...

I didn't see you there.

This is not what I imagined

This is not what I imagined
When I held you in my arms;
So small and full of promise
Now I guard you from self-harm

I look down at your photographs
A toddler smiles from ear to ear
I couldn't see the mask then
That you hid behind for years

We played and had adventures
Laughed together in the park
Cozy, snuggly bedtimes
Before we both cried in the dark

We didn't see it coming
It swept in aggressively
Consuming you before my eyes
My child lost to me

It goes by many guises
They share many common traits
Fear, pain and isolation
Breeding conflict, growing hate

So, I hid away the photos
Couldn't listen to our songs
Donned a shell, forged some armour
Carved a new version of 'strong'

Couldn't pull you from its clutches
Couldn't free you from its claws
Had to turn around and face myself
Challenge my ideas and flaws

Endless emails and phone calls
Reading blogs and books and posts
All the while holding you
Fighting demons, evil ghosts

Learning that this road is long
No shortcuts here or cheats
For each small success and victory
You will endure defeats

But with time, now armed with knowledge
And having found you some support
Those photos they can bring you hope
They're not lies as we once thought

All those happy memories
The laughter that we shared
The footprints in the sand we made
In fact, they're all still there

And one day in the future
Though it may not be tomorrow
Those memories will light your spark
And quell your fears and sorrow

You may not do all of the things
You did easily before
This illness has brought change in you
But you're not less my love, you're more

To fight the way that you have done
And still do every day
Takes strength and power deep inside
Through the dark you found your way

We now accept days differently
Monday's smooth then Tuesday's rough
But gradually you dare to dream
Learning that you are enough

This is not what I imagined
I've seen my child torn apart
This illness takes no prisoners
Can break the strongest heart

But it didn't count on something
Didn't count on you and I
It thought that it had taken you
The days you asked to die

It took you to the darkest place
Couldn't see a path ahead
Dwelling in that darkness
I kept guard beside your bed

In the wee small hours
I found solace in a book
A community of shared grief and hope
If you just know where to look

With our shared determination
We saw glimmers, saw some light
Diagnosis, validation
With understanding we could fight

This journey has to be your own
I root for you inside
No, it's not what I imagined
And yet I feel such pride

This is not what I imagined
You are more, oh so much more
Of your bravery and strength my love
I'm utterly in awe

I see how you grow daily
Emerging from the dark
some days we sing our songs again
And laugh together in the park.

In memory and celebration of Kharmahn and others no longer with us but always in our hearts.

OCD I hate you

OCD. I hate you.

I hate how you tighten your stealth like grip around my son. How you rob him of his freedom to play and venture outdoors and show affection. I hate how you fill his head with your lies and threats so that his hands and heart bear your scars. I hate how you alienate him from those he loves and how you steal from him his education as your tendrils reach beyond our home and follow him. Always there. I hate how you leave your footprints on his heart and mine. How you leave your handprints on my home…watermarks on the ceiling from the flooded bathroom floor…the 5th shower because it wasn't exactly right, the huge gas bill that smirks up at me from the page, laughing at the hot water that was demanded by you, the heating to dry his clothes as they had to be washed again at your command. The empty bottles of soap that collect on the shelf are your trophies you flaunt to display your power and control.

OCD I hate you.

At times I'm guilty of forgetting that it's your voice that screams abuse at me from the shower, your words that hurt and cut to the core "I'm not fighting a battle mum I'm fighting a war". My sweet boy. But you have hijacked him OCD until sometimes I can't see him anymore.

Only you as he valiantly fights you every minute of every, exhausting day. Until bedtime when he must check you won't brutally kill him as he sleeps.

OCD I hate you.

You stole our bedtime closeness, our cosy chats. You took them and stamped your fear all over.

And then, one day, a triumph. A small step. A little less soap. And I'm reminded that my son will beat you. Maybe not just yet. But he will.

OCD I hate you. But I love my son, he is brave and strong and true.

Not like you. Love will win. One day...

Music stops, silence falls

Was thinking yesterday about how many kids use music as a way to escape or to empower?
Toby has a school run playlist. It's pretty brutal listening. Sometimes they'll go for light hearted dance or 80's (eclectic tastes) but when the really offensive loud stuff goes on, I know they're struggling and this is their way of readying themselves for what lies ahead. I ignore the judgemental glances of other school mum drivers; this is important and it seems to help.
I wrote this piece about that journey...

Music...loud, explicit, offensive swearing,

Rebellion blaring. The armour goes on to the beat of the song, speakers vibrating, fists clenched and shaking...a haka-like ritual

Fierce, strong and powerful...

School bag on shoulder, face stoic, now bolder, the music stops pounding
But the feelings surrounding
Uncensored, no rules, it prepared him for school.

A routine of his making, it stops him from shaking…

They'll see defiant and ready (though he's scared and unsteady) through the gate, chin held high...they'll not see him cry.

Music stops, silence falls
He walked into school.

♥

The tale of the lonely lunch box

He sits alone in the kitchen. His bulging sides poignantly revealing that his contents are uneaten, untouched. His destiny denied again.

Not all days start this way.
On some days the boy comes in and grabs the yellow strap, and they venture forth together.

But not today.
Not today.

On those days he snuggles safely in the boy's back pack. Often listening with growing fury to the persecution and punishments, wishing he had fists. Baffled by this place they call school. If they make it to lunchtime, he can then take pride in knowing that momentarily he does a vital job. He gives the boy familiarity, comfort and connection.
Food for the tummy
Sustenance for the soul.

Some days the food is enjoyed at leisure. The other lunchboxes mingle on the table and the chatter of their owners fills the air. The boy smiles but barely eats, hurriedly biting into bread, eager to zip up and run, in the sun with the others.
Then there are the lunchtimes filled with the loudest of silences.

Distant, incoherent shouts of happy voices sometimes pierce the solemn quiet. There are no other lunchboxes here.

The boy sits alone. Each piece of food means more on those days, flavours bring comfort, reminders of home. The vibrant pattern, familiar images of playful dogs in bright jackets make him smile. A little. So, he makes up a story about those dogs and speaks it aloud between mouthfuls, comforting himself, filling the silence.

The guard arrives, named teacher and indicates seclusion is over. Time is served, lunch is finished. No play today. Lunchbox stuffed back into school bag hoping it has done enough. Knowing he hasn't, he can't make this better, he is but a lunchbox after all.

How can he shout the boy's truth to those who would listen? To voice his sadness at the broken trust and hurtful comments he endures from those named 'staff'.
He is no advocate; he is just a lunchbox.

Yet somehow he knows he has a purpose here, he fills a void, especially on a no play day.

But not today.

Today he sits alone in the kitchen. The clock ticks on, mocking, goading. 'Staying home again? It's getting late…traffic building, you should be on your way'

He turns away, willing the boy to come bounding into the kitchen, but his hopes are in vain.

In truth he knows.

He knew last night as he watched the tear-stained mother chop carrot sticks at midnight. Dark eyed with exhaustion from the bedtime struggles. Brows stroked, feet rubbed, stories told, silly songs sung to comfort and distract from the 'night terrors' whatever they may be. Relations of 'the staff' perhaps? Her tears had fallen dampening the breadsticks and were quickly replaced with fresh ones, in little plastic boxes and placed inside. An apple, a brioche (the boy detests sandwiches) carrots, strawberries, granola bar and sometimes pizza or a pancake. Always a note.

Damn that note, it always made the mother cry as she placed it inside, which confused him somewhat as the same note always made the boy smile, even momentarily.

The lunchbox filled, poised, anticipating adventure and ready to comfort him in her absence.

But not today.

He had watched as she appeared again, bleary eyes and seeking coffee. Stealing herself to wake the boy. Maybe today...

But it wasn't to be.

"I want to but I can't"
His words echo down the stairs and drift into the kitchen.
"I'm too anxious, they don't understand me there, they punish me, I can't do it again"
He knew not what these words meant, but he knew that today there would be no play or solitary comforts shared.

The mother would come in time and remove his contents. She may discard them or if feeling hopeful she may store them in the fridge in readiness for the next day. Maybe tomorrow. Yes maybe tomorrow the lunchbox would go. But today he sits alone in the kitchen. The world carries on.

Children chatter and play on their way to school. Parents complain about traffic...whatever that is.
The mother would love to be in traffic...but not today.
Yes the world carries on today, like so many others but the boy sits alone at home.

And the lunchbox sits alone in the kitchen. The mother cannot bear to banish him to the cupboard, that would be too final, too much.

Because you see, all the while he sits there in the kitchen, waiting, he is a tiny beacon of hope to her.

We will try again…

Tomorrow.

There's always you

When I feel alone
Scrolling through my contacts
Don't know who to call
To burden
To reach out to....

There's always you.

You don't judge
Or push, criticise, dismiss
Or pry
When I cry.

You wait silently
Patiently
Holding space
For me
Until the tears subside
And I can breathe

You listen
While I share the 'our truth'
Murmuring words of comfort
And solidarity
Validation
And love.

And above all else
In those broken moments
I know I am not alone
And I am blessed

Because there's always you.
(Lou)

Anecdotes from Neurodivergent family life...

2-3 Business Days

Me: I'm wondering if you'd rather go out the following weekend instead of next week? There are a lot of events on, so it may be very busy. Just a thought.

Daughter: I will need to give it some thought. I shall respond in approximately 2 to 3 business days.

After a challenging day of managing separation anxiety whilst I supported my youngest at their taster day for new provision, I made my daughter some hot buttered toast. I'd tidied her room a little and made sure her favourite pj's were ready after her bath (with a bit of Bath bomb in to relax)

She just came into my room...

"Thank you for the toast, I revel in the little things you do for me. I did a happy dance after you left."

"You're welcome my love; I always try to do little things when you're dealing with big things" "You do, and I'm very appreciative. And sometimes they warrant a happy dance "

The journey to the therapy farm is never dull.

Conversation starters in today's 25 minute trip were as follows...

1. I'm pretty sure I saw a wasp ejaculate today. It was thrusting up and down then there was a liquid, so I'm drawing a natural conclusion.
2. Why are their Drs called Gynaecologists? Considering

their area of expertise, they really should be called Vaginacologists.
3. You see a lot of people with hairy hands these days.
4. If someone gets pregnant from a sperm donor but has never had sex, did they even lose their virginity?
5. I have very eclectic musical tastes (switches to yungblud from Dolly Parton)
6. It makes me sad to see that homeless man. I'd like to give him my Croissant but there's nowhere to stop. In all honesty he'd probably prefer cash but a Croissant is better than nothing.
7. BANG (very loudly, intermittently, frequently whilst I'm reversing or at a junction) Nope, never dull.

A little context:

At this point, we were rarely able to go out for any distance or length of time. We couldn't leave her sibling. But today, we had a plan B.
We were heading to Greenwich, one of our favourite happy places. Inspired by her style and poise, I had decided to be brave.
I had put on make-up, jeans and a leather jacket.
Looking in the mirror I felt like me, for the first time in a long, long time.
Her: Mum you look fantastic
Me: Not too 'young' for me?

Her: Don't be ridiculous.
You look like you.
You look like a rock chick.
Your hair is soft, your boots are hard.
You look like how I imagine one of your emails would look if they were personified. A thing of beauty with an air of don't fuck with me!

God how I loved her in that moment.
And always.

―――――

When you're shattered; you've cleaned and tidied the kitchen,
You're on the home stretch to bedtime...
Then you're youngest (who rarely steps away from the PC screen - as gaming is their coping strategy for OCD and PTSD) says:
" I know it's late, so you'll probably say no, but would you like to make pancakes together, from scratch, because we haven't cooked together for ages because of the OCD"
Needless to say, the whisk was out in seconds!
And it wasn't uneventful…the Tics combined with eggs and flour are an interesting dynamic...but we did it.
Pancakes flipped! And they danced. And smiled.
And better than Nutella, or sugar and lemon...on top of pancakes, I got a big hug. ❤🥞🥞🥞

Daughter:

I had a great time in Rye mum, we had Panna cotta ice cream and looked at the visitors centre but dad wouldn't let me buy a gun! Or a dagger, they were so ornate and beautiful mum.

Husband:

I am not bringing you home from our first day trip for ages with an arsenal of weaponry!

At bedtime…late

"I need to find the peace pocket."
"Peace pocket?"
"Yes; it's the little place in my mind I put tranquil, calm things to think about. Which distracts me from the total chaos that is my

brain"

"Ok"

"Yes; I will put the small-holding and the chicken called Motherclucker in there."

Mother's meltdown

Adrenalin pumping.

Nausea rising.

Sweating.

Panting.

Hyperventilating.

Stomach cramping.

Fingers clawing.

Scratching.

Marking.

Containing

Containing

The swearing

The shouting

The crying

The feeling

Swallowing

Smiling

Blinking (to stop the crying)

Helping

Supporting

Partnering

Them through the dark.

So, they're not alone.

(Whilst you mask,
Contain,
And hide
Your own)

The broken hangers

Under her pillow
Though barely concealed
I find the broken hangers
Staring up at me
Telling me of her pain.

One is twisted
Must have taken some force
Distorted almost beyond recognition
It tells of grief,
Of frustration,
And angst

The other snapped clean
In several places
Shards of plastic now jigsaw pieces
That together reveal the picture
The full force of feeling.
Needing to break,
To snap
Not just in two,
But...
Again
and again.

I see in my hands her expression of pain,
This was her way of coping with what felt so raw,
When I had to go,
to leave her,
For just a short while.
Guilt tightens it's vice like grip around my chest.

I had to go, for a short while today,

I had to trust that our plan was enough.
These twisted hangers,
The pain that shaped them, the legacy of the trauma that makes her cling to the safety that I represent.
Ever present.

Yet we both know,
(She is wise beyond words)
That sometimes I must leave her,
to help,
I must go,
 away.
For just a short while,
Believing in her, even when she doubts herself,
That she's got this.

We've built the reserves
We've talked through her plan

"Distractions"

" strategies "

Sometimes it feels like we converse solely in words to articulate either pain, or ways to manage it.

But it is what is it.
We have to embrace the darkness
Swim the murky depths together
If she is to find her way to the surface.

She wears on her wrist
Her warrior cuff
letters spelling out
That she
is
enough.

Today the broken hangers
Were stuffed beneath the pillow.
And what followed?

She went out!
Without me
And bought plants that sit now on her window sill.
The scent of herbs to flood her senses and soothe her soul,
A testament to her strength,
Her courage,

My warrior daughter...

I look down at the fragments of plastic.
The hangers that were,
I turn them over in my hands
Run my fingers along their edges,
And I smile.
Not a joyous smile
But one of acceptance,
Of relief,
and yes, of pride.

She found healing release didn't keep this
Inside.

Stripped bare

Dehumanising

For them, of course for them
But also, for you.

It strips away your dignity
Autonomy
Until one day you find yourself hiding in your bedroom.
Using a plastic container as a toilet because your child is hauled up in the bathroom
Frozen there by angst, anxiety,
demand avoidance.

They cannot come out, because you need them to.

And after a day of meeting needs, and staying calm and neutral as the latest tirade of insults is flung your way,
You sob into your duvet.
Desperate for rest but stuck waiting again.
Praying for the flush to signal they're moving on to the shower…the next ritual…one step closer to bed.

But instead, you're clutching your stomach and hoping you can hang on.
Your mind so fogged by tiredness, too many tabs open, you

absentmindedly ate the chicken that had been sitting out all day. And now you feel really sick.

But you can't get into the bathroom
And they can't come out

Because you need them to.
Catch-22

So, you wait. And you cry.
Feeling like a child,
In pain,
Unable to meet the most basic of human needs for yourself.

You feel less of a woman.
Hiding these ugly scenes.
You feel shame.
Stripped bare.
You can't share,

This side
Of caring for a child with mental illness

From the kitchen floor

I seem to find myself here often.
The kitchen floor.
In a ball.
In the corner.
 Looking up at the sky
Framed by the wide kitchen window.

Clouds today.
Vast expanse of grey
Reflecting the heaviness of my heart.
The weight of the darkness in my chest.
And a solitary black bird
Gliding past.

From here I can reach for a tea towel
To muffle my sobs
And bury my head against the vegetable cupboard.
When my legs can't hold me.
The kitchen floor can
For a while.

Sometimes it catches me unaware
A sudden sadness
Triggered by a song,
An email,

A memory,
And sometimes it's a heaviness I've carried all day
That finally swells and refuses
To be ignored.

But even here I can't hide.
From the weight of responsibility, tasks that overwhelm me.
Paperwork to do.
Not just bills
But the stuff of great significance.

Advocating exhausting.
The timelines
Going over emails in intricate detail
Formulating a plan
Gathering evidence
Knowing that much of my child's happiness
And future prospects Is riding on me
Getting
This
Right.

And meanwhile
The dishes
And the laundry
(The single label- free pair of pjs they'll wear)
Must be clean and dry

Or meltdowns will erupt
They need to right clothes
At the right time
To feel safe
And settled.

And I listen for any escalation in their voice
As they talk online
Subtle nuances in tone
Alerting me to a building storm...
But for now
They're calm

Replay the morning
Events that left me feeling even more hollow.
Less of a person.
A woman.
More a service
There to meet the needs of others.
Never mind my own.
Now he's gone to work
I reflect from the kitchen floor and feel even greater sadness.
And I know
It's not ok

But I can't deal with it
Not today

And he apologised
So, I'll leave it
Brush over it

Until the next time.

And I can't talk about it.
Everyone's at work.
And as I scroll
I know that as my number flashes up
They'll roll their eyes
And let it ring out
Not today.
Too much.

So, I don't.
Instead, I sob into the damp tea-towel
And sometimes
Bang my head
Gently,
Rhythmically
against the vegetable cupboard.
To feel something other
Than the weight of the load
I
Carry.

And then I stop.
 I wipe my eyes
And I stand up.
The dishes won't do themselves.

And I have to be strong.
Have been for so long.
I've had my moment of self-indulgent
Vulnerability.
No room for more.
Can't stay on the floor.

So, I stand
And load the washing machine.
Knowing that my efforts are seen.
By them
The ones who matter.
My children.

How can I help them to stand tall?
From the kitchen floor?

I open my notebook
 I open my phone
And begin the next email.

The next form

The next appeal.

This is the real me.

And knowing they see I will always

Fight their corner

Is enough

To help me get up again

From mine

On the kitchen floor.

And so it begins

And so, it begins...
Back to school

We watch as the familiar feeling of dread envelops us. We watch as our children's sparkle, their glimmer of light, dulls just a little more each day. We watch the billboard Ads and uniform posts and see the frantic mothers dashing to the shoe store...the stationary store. Their biggest worry that their child will not have the right attire. We watch, knowing that this is where it all begins again...

We listen, we listen to the mothers, telling tales of sun-kissed summer adventures. Of sandcastles, seasides and smiles. We listen to the voices laced with giddy excitement...the children keen to see their friends, the parents 'exhausted' from uploading another photo montage of their happy, smiling insta perfect family...enjoying another happy, smiling, insta-perfect daytrip...congratulating each other on 'surviving summer' with the kids. We listen with envy as they share the chores they'll be heading home to...washing out sandy buckets and tidying away the treasures their children collected on their many adventures. We listen to the sigh of relief as 'back to school day' approaches...they'll post their picture-perfect uniform snap.

We hide, hide behind smiles and the well-rehearsed facade we have cultivated over years of struggle and strength. Smiling, as mothers discuss the shiny pencil case (we have one of those) or correct gym kit...or how glad they are to wave off their children at last, safe in the knowledge that they'll have a great day, a safe day.

We hide from our heartbreak, to feel it would make it impossible to hold on. And we have to hold on.

We hold on as we are the safe space, we are the watchers. We look, look for the glimmers of light imperceptible to others. In the absence of summer fun days, we look for the little moments we have come to treasure. A brief smile, ten minutes in the garden, a meltdown free morning...these are our 'insta' moments, our reasons smile. Will we lose that glimmer as the 'back to school' anxiety hits home?

So, we plan, plan and prepare. We steal ourselves for battle and despite all the previous failings we hope, we hope this year will be different. We hope that this year our children will do more than simply survive. We hope and we email CAMHS, school, attendance officer, GP...we call, we ask.

We ask that they support our children. Support our children as they go 'back to school' with accommodations, with care, understanding and with kindness.

We ask for kindness. We ask for kindness.

And as the day draws near, we navigate the insomnia of our children, borne from anxiety we cradle them in the aftermath of another ferocious meltdown and we reassure them with all the belief we can muster, that this year will be different. We remove labels from clothes, we rewash uniform to ensure it smells 'right' and we talk through visuals of our morning routine. We have breakfast menus A, B and C all at the ready and alternative outfits washed and waiting in the wings. Like a well-staged production, choreographed to pack in all the 'feel good' we can before school. We play their favourite songs and drive their preferred route. We do all we can, knowing that it'll never be fool proof but it might just be enough today. On Back-to-school day.

And suddenly (we didn't see it coming) we crumple. Overwhelmed by the conflicting emotions that swell from our very stomachs and catch in our throats.

Relief...we did it, they went Back to school...they're walking away...

But did we do the right thing? Will their sparkle survive another day or be extinguished by lunchtime?

Fear, will they be ok? Will they be alone, lonely? Treated with compassion? Do the staff understand co regulation? They can't do it alone yet will they know when they are simmering?

Admiration, pride and awe the bravery and guts they have astounds us. They are the warriors...

Dread, dread of the after-school collapse. We are already anticipating the impact of 6 hours of masking, peopling and expectations. Armour at the ready...

And sometimes, some days...
Simply acceptance laced with sadness ours didn't make it 'Back-to-school' and that's ok, it'll be ok. They weren't ready today. Today we will nurture the glimmer of light. And try again. Or try something else, somewhere else.

The shiny pencil case, the SENDCo calls, the label-less clothing...
And so, it begins.

Outside the bathroom door

I sit outside the bathroom door.
On the floor.
Waiting.
Listening.

Wrestling with the urge to speak, to engage.
It's ok as long as I can hear them.
I can hear them.
Watching memes and scrolling.
The fast-paced flicker a means of distraction from the racing thoughts.
The screaming has stopped for now.
The rage subdued but I'm mindful it can return with avengeance like the flick of a switch.
If I say the wrong thing. If I say anything.

So, I sit outside the bathroom door.
Waiting.
Listening.

My eyes wander to the dust on the skirting board.
Silently judging myself for its presence.
I notice the marks on the wall and the tiny tear in the wallpaper.
They are gloating, mocking my existence and what my life has become.

Can't even keep house, can you? Don't work. Did you even brush your hair today?"

I close my eyes and breathe. I can't cry. Not now. This is not about me or my lost autonomy.

I hear them move. Hear a YouTube video playing.
Fight the urge to tell them dinner is ready (in fact, dinner is ruined. It was ready thirty minutes ago when the meltdown started. Now its black and tough as rubber) in an attempt to coax them out. It doesn't work. They need space. They need the world to pause long enough for them to catch their breath. So, I pause with them. To keep them safe.

Like a sentry I sit outside the bathroom door and wait.
I reach for my phone. Still waiting I open emails. Searching. Hoping. No email from school.
Further disappointment and broken promises for them as I anticipate the question later. "Did school email mum?"

This won't be the last meltdown today. My heart breaks a little more.

And I sit outside the bathroom door, on the floor.
Waiting.
Xx

It's not about the ice cream

A crumpled mess, my hair, my clothes.
Me.
A slightly comical figure as I sob, on the floor,
gasping to catch my breathe.
Over Ice cream.
And cereal.

The no branded cereal.
The wrong type of Ice cream.
It's not what I asked for.
You decided another brand would do.
You.

Sound like a spoiled child?
I'm not. I'm wild.
And sad.
I can't shop for my ice cream
Or cereal
This is my real
Life.

Day in
Day out.
I'm here.
Holding ground

Holding hands

Holding hearts

Can't leave them, or be apart

So don't tell me 'Don't start'

Because I didn't get to buy my ice cream.

Or my cereal.

Anecdotes from Neurodivergent family life…

The other day we went out to walk the dogs. Daughter looked stunning in bright red lipstick and her Cath Kidston handbag shaped like a cloud with a rainbow strap.

Me: Love your look honey

Daughter: It's symbolic (has been studying WW2- for context)
The lipstick is because the Wrens started wearing red as a F@#k you to Hitler as make up and bright colours were frowned upon by the Nazi regime. They chose the brightest red.
The bag is a f#@k you to misogynistic individuals who claim women have their heads in the clouds.
The strap is a bit of LGBTQ+ thrown in because hey, I think I just like everyone. Ok.

———

Conversations with my daughter today...

Me: you're trying to carry a lot there, I'm coming upstairs behind you, can I help at all?
D: No.
Me: OK
D: I'm sorry, it's just that I'm a rather determined bast@#d

D: Damn this flouncy skirt, it's impossible to walk upstairs. I shall have to walk like an ogre.

D: Oh no, I'm wearing blue and white. People might think I've dressed up for the Jubilee. I need a badge stating that I'm not a raging royalist.

D: Look at that truck mum, I really love it.
Me: Nice Matt grey finish yeah.
D: No, I mean it's big and sturdy. You could like run 4 people over at once.
Me: Would you want to, though?
D: Don't be naive mother, we need to prepare for the apocalypse.

It's never dull!!

———

Daughter: Look, I would really appreciate you hearing me out. It's not like I'm asking for the earth. Just a Dwarf Nigerian Pygmy Goat. Called Carl.

———

Do you like my tousled curls? I'm going for a whimsical look today!

———

D: Do you remember in the long lockdown. When it was summer, we saw two butterflies in the garden having sex?
Me: No, I don't remember that.
D: Don't worry, it was interesting so I filmed it. Not sure I want to

watch it though; wouldn't that be butterfly porn?

———

I have come to the conclusion that some eggs are co-operative and others aren't. Some are willing to go with it and curl contentedly into a ball when you poach them, but others are determined to foil their fate and spread like a starfish.
I hate those eggs.

The shower

I remembered today.
The time I climbed into the shower.
I don't recall the trigger
Or what came before.
Just you
On the floor
Of the shower
Asking to die.

I seem to remember
It had been a school day
A day of flashbacks
And navigating current storms
As well as past demons.

You were so tired
Weary of the fight
You just sat with water cascading
Over your battered heart
And you cried.
Tears of frustration and hurt.
Tears of exhaustion.
Asking me to make it stop.

You said you couldn't fight
Had nothing left
Just too worn down worn out.
Wanted peace.

So, I stayed with you.
On the floor
The other side of the shower
door
Watching the water trickle
Over your crimson brow.
And asked myself
How did we get here?

And all at once
You looked so small
And I knew what to do.
It wasn't enough to offer
platitudes
From behind a shower screen
Or try to pull you from this hole.

I needed to get into the hole.
With you.

So, I offered you a hug.
 You looked so confused,

Reminded me I was fully
dressed.
I offered again.
And a glimmer of a smile flickered briefly across
your face.

You nodded
And I climbed into the shower
beside you.
And I held you
Your head in my lap
As the water ran down my neck
And we stayed there.

Until together
We stood up.

And you asked if you could wash my hair..
Suds and shampoo
Your fingers on my head
Jeans plastered to my legs

" Are you going anywhere on your holidays
madam?" You were joking.
And smiling.

The storm had passed for now.

Yes I remember

When you wanted to go, because you

Had no fight left to stand alone

You needed me to show you,

You didn't have to.

And I knew

I'd always remember the time I climbed into the shower.

Blazer in a bin bag

Today I fold the clothes
Put away the uniform
Not neatly, in readiness for Monday
But forever.

It's over.
Gone.
Finished.
We're done.
Blazer in a binbag,
Photos torn down.
No need for the lunch bag,
School shoes can go
To where?
I don't know.

Our path changed by their failings,
Not just in training,
But in kindness, compassion,
No passion ...
For change.

So;
It's over.
They've forced our hand,

Left us no choice
But to go.

We saw it coming.
For months.
The meetings,
So futile,
But all the while,
We tried, goodness we tried
'Parental engagement'
Guidance from CAMHS
More emails
and phone calls
Unread and unheard

This system's absurd.

The tears and the trauma
Meltdown and pain
The dents in the door
A heart on the floor

Until something had to give
For you to live.

Then an escalation
We weren't ready for this.

"That's misgendering"
"Whatever!"
Pain dismissed

'Keep them home for their safety'
You said…

Because school made them feel that they wished they were dead.
Because school made them feel that they wished they were dead.

It never would have worked.
They simply couldn't see you.
And no matter how we tried
They simply wouldn't hear you

In your fear
They saw hostility
In your jokes
Insolence
No sense, in staying.

Their barked 'warnings'
Simply fanned the flames
Of your hurt
Of your fury.

Then they watched you burn.
Then they watched you burn.

Tears of frustration
For a punishment
And another
And another

Missed breaktime
They couldn't take time to talk to you.
"Just think it through"
(You sipped your tea, ate your lunch.
No support for 'reflection'
The angst led to a punch)

"Your child has ADHD
They'll get detentions"
At this, a 'Special School'
Did I mention?
Tone policing
"You're rude!"
"You cannot say that"
 Go outside
Take 'a break'
(What a fake)
"But don't climb or run
Or have fun.

Stand there, in that bay
That's where you must stay
Or detention for you"

Then the most ironic sanction of all
Three days of Isolation
Named 'An Inclusion'
In this 'Special School'

So enough.
They've done enough
Damage.
You called them out!
So proud to hear you shout
Autism, ADHD
They are me; don't you see?

Eloquently listing
Their failings
Their flaws
You faced them
And you told them
"I won't take it anymore"

"It's lies, all lies
You and your rules
I'm not welcome in your school"

That magic 'drop mic' moment
Left me breathless and in awe
Pivotal and poignant
A child's voice no more.

"You didn't want to understand me
You didn't even try
Just crushed me with your punishments
So I'm leaving now
Goodbye"

So today we put away the clothes
And all things school
Their blanket policies
Their rules...
A new beginning today
 Not through choice its true
But a change,
Could be good?
For you.

Our CAMHS comrade had said
 And she's right, it was true.
At 14 you chose Mental Health,

Brave enough to choose you! 🖤🖤🖤

Proud just doesn't cover it
The way you stood tall
But the pain that it came from
Will stay with us all.

So as we start a new chapter
You carve a new path

[Those who have failed you
The uncaring staff...
This isn't over,
I'm coming for you!
Through all the right channels
And they'll know our truth.]

The unthinkable

I know I'm not alone thinking or feeling this way.
I've read others voicing their thoughts
And silently judged them.
In denial.
I will never think that way!

But right here, right now
I understand in a way
I never imagined possible.

And I don't know the person I've become
Who am I to think these thoughts?

You see it goes against every natural instinct of my being.
The thread from which I'm woven.
Made to shield, nurture and protect

With my very life.

My heart beats for them.
My child.
But they are not my child anymore.
This illness stole them and replaced them with this tyrant.
Whom I can never, ever, appease.
My Mr Hyde

In any other guise my friends and family
Would tell me to leave.
Question my sanity for staying and enduring
Day after day.

A sign a weakness?
Broken spirit.
Martyr!
Weak!
But no one speaks of this.
It's a secret.
Don't tell.
They'll bring in the professionals.
Or send you on a course
Or tell you how well you're coping.

They have no clue
About you.

Praying for bedtime,
And dreading it.
Because I can never truly rest
Knowing that tomorrow it all begins again.

Hiding my pain as I try to open a jar

And can't.

Damaged thumb.

Possibly broken.

My fault though.

They told me at the time.

Yelling unrepentantly

That it would teach me.

(I mismanaged the rage)

"YOU GOT IN MY FACE,

YOU GOT IN THE WAY!"

I got in the way.

A glancing blow,

Mr Hyde in full flow with such force,

For one

So slight.

And it's strange,

But that searing pain

Was somehow easier to bear

Than the shame.

And every day

I lose a little more of myself.

Of my marriage

My daughter

Of my soul.

It dies slowly.

Beaten down by the constant and unrelenting demands.

And abuse.

(Mostly verbal

Sometimes physical.)

Words I never dreamed would cross the lips

Of my darling child.

The egg shell walk

From dawn till dusk.

Don't step on the cracks!

But it's never enough.

I am never enough.

And in my tired fog I stumble

Or mumble...

My voice silenced

"DON'T YOU DARE SPEAK"

My appearance changed

"I can't handle make up

You look different

I hate it"

YOU DO IT ON PURPOSE TO HURT ME!

And the words wash over me

Trickle into my being

And drown my heart all over again.

I look

For the hope.

For the glimmer of light

The life buoy

And some days it comes

But others are dark.

And so, it goes on.

And on.

Until one day

You're so broken

You're done.

"Please take them someone!"

You think it

And expect the door to crash in

As the police come

To cart you away.

But

Nothing

Happens.

And as time goes on,

Without change

It becomes easier to say
And think.

Never so they'll hear
(Just when you're alone)
Crying over your phone
Or book
That tells you
It's OK
It's PDA.

And you know you have to carry on.
And stay.

It's the illness
Not your child.

It's the illness.

I HATE YOU

It's the illness.

YOU'RE F%#%ING USELESS

It's the illness.

YOU STUPID COW

It's the illness

I say it again and again
As though it's an incantation
That will magically
restore my sight
And help me
To see my child
Again.

But there is no magic.

Just a weary mother
Putting one foot
In front of another
Whilst smiling for her daughter
(Must protect her, my dearest, dearest love)
And cooking for her husband
(Marriages fail if not nurtured…he has needs you know)
Close the door
And
Keep spinning
The
Plates.

In the hope

That perhaps

Sometime soon

The good days

May begin

To out number

The bad.

And Dr Jekyll

Might find that pill

And I will

See my child again.

Lost

There was once a woman.

She wore dark, dusky pink lipstick

And perfume.

Snug fitting, smart skirts with funky prints

And heeled brown boots.

She wore a lanyard.

Her picture smiling back from the photocard.

Her name.

Her position.

There in black and white.

She was liked

By fellow staff and the children she helped.

She smiled a lot.

But her child

Did not.

So there came a day

When the woman had to take the lanyard off.

And give it back.

And walk away.

Away from a part of herself.

From what defined her
In so many ways

Away from the lipstick
And skirts and boots
And the respect of colleagues
And the smile.
Away from the perfume.
Away from autonomy
From routine and from normalcy
And it scared the woman.

Who was she without her work?
A housewife?
She was no good at that.
Try as she might the things
That came easily to others,
Were a challenge for her to manage.

Overwhelmed by the seemingly never ending
Chores.
Chasing her tail,
Playing catch up on laundry, dishes, cleaning...
When do people even wash their skirting boards?
A mother? Yes, a mother.
But even that role seemed to constantly
Change in description, requirements, Job spec.

With this new way of being,
This crisis life,
The sense of security she had once felt,
Conviction of her decisions
Eluded her.

The woman wore leggings
And sweaters for warmth.
She seemed to always feel tired
And cold
And old.
No point wearing lipstick.
Or boots.
Her bare feet became hardened
From never wearing shoes.

Her work place, her home
Meshed into one
But she didn't feel competent
In either role.
The illness stole,
Her children,
Her husband,
(Couldn't be the wife she was meant to be
Although he'd never have said as much)
And her identity.

And in this way

It continued

Her story

Her life

As the woman grappled with finding a new direction.

A way to be

Her.

She became hardened round the edges

No longer soft to touch.

(Survival does that to a person)

As she fought off the demons that would've swallowed her children whole.

The system,

School,

Timetables,

Rules.

The woman,

She realised,

That the way she had been led to believe was right,

Might in fact,

Not be.

Her family

Would be treading a new path

And she would need to find the way.

Compass at the ready.

And thus began her new story.

The woman still wears leggings

Or sometimes a dress

With her hair now pinned up

With a splash of colour here and there.

Her life has a renewed sense of direction

Which is far from easy

(And she frequently still gets lost)

But,

She realises that sometimes,

Although risky, and laced with peril,

The path less travelled,

Boasts a wonderful view.

And a different way,

To be you.

A birthday - Pt 1

A Birthday you say?

A day where routines are different, so anxiety spirals from the start?

And expectations to be 'good' increase pressure even further and cause meltdowns which you then need to support through and navigate?

And presents from some, who try so hard, serve to intensify the hurt at the absence of others. For whom your Birthday wasn't really important.

Only they then feel bad and decide they want to make an effort to celebrate...but only on their terms, doing what they want to do, when they want to do it, and if you argue, (because despite it being your Birthday you have an important EHCP meeting at 11am) you're rejecting their efforts!

And you're still expected to locate the sodding Sellotape.
A Birthday you say?
No thanks. I'll pass.

A birthday - Pt 2

I survived my Birthday!

This morning, in the wee small hours,
I sat in a ball, on my kitchen floor
Sobbing.
I felt like I was 5.
"I don't want a Birthday"
Was my mantra, through the tears.

Until my head could take no more.
I got up from the floor
And went to bed
For a few restless hours.

There were some golden moments that day,
Which fought back against the darkness

The daylight brought coffee.
I decided to embrace the day as best I could,
Despite the card from my husband staring up at me,
bearing an image of the kind of woman I am not,
nor will ever be.

Just not me.

There were some treasures
Some beautiful, bright moments.
The poem written by my daughter,
Given with such tenderness and love
Her words a treasured gift,
Literally made my heart sing.
She spoke of admiration,
my ferocity and strength

I would go to any lengths
For her.

The OCD challenge my youngest triumphantly achieved,
stepping into the garden and returning without seeking solace in the shower.
For an hour.
"I'm doing it for you mum"

Birthday treats have become
Somewhat different
Somewhat new.
It's true.

The cards and gifts from my husband, from friends,
so thoughtful and kind,
A bright, vibrant testimony
They were thinking of me.

So, I survived my Birthday
And more than that,
I learned at the ripe age of 45
That as long as we are alive...

There can be change

(And maybe Birthdays aren't so bad.)

Footprints in the sand

I miss them.

Foot prints in the sand...

Feet sinking

Toes curling

Waves crashing

Washing over our toes.

As we are busy making footprints

And memories

With Sea air

Wind in hair

Smiling girls

Wide open world

Footprints gone

Washed away by the tide

We can't make anymore

Can't go outside

And although washed away

They'll stay

Etched in my mind

To sustain through this time

And I know

That one day

We will go

and make more

Footprints in the sand.

Anecdotes from Neurodivergent family life…

So, it's very, very rare these days, and for a long while actually, that I get embarrassed. As long as no harm is caused, my children are encouraged to be their authentic selves. Sod what other people think.

My children are both fabulous, eccentric and sometimes perceived as 'rude' as they often don't adhere to what's socially acceptable (in varying degrees)

Today as we drove home from the farm, my Youngest was very happy. In a celebratory mood even. So, we had VERY loud music playing on the journey.

At one point, the flow of traffic stopped outside a church, where people were leaving a funeral.

With no malice intended, Youngest says 'I've got just the tune for that!" And proceeds to play the Yungblud, The Funeral song at Full, window rattling, bone shaking volume.

For context, this is a feel-good song for them, which they sing loudly to when happy or excited. It helps them feel better if they're sad, and celebrate too.

So the traffic starts moving (much to my relief) only very slowly...
I then realise we are now in the funeral procession, with mourners, including church ministers, walking alongside us. Slowly.

As we blast Funeral.

Very,

Very

Loudly.

But I couldn't and wouldn't put a stop to it. Because the mourners seemed oblivious (apart from a sweet old lady who clocked the ' I've got a fuc#ed up soul and an STD' lyric as she crossed the road!) And my YP was endeavouring to share their joy!
In their own, authentic way.
It was a scene straight out of a sitcom, that's our life!

Me: What are you wearing on your feet and as a jacket today?
D: Fury and anarchy
Me: Ok

Gem of the day... From the bathroom..
"Mum, you know sometimes these parts get referred to as meat and two veg?"
"Well, yes"
" Well, what about Vegans?"
" Errrrr"
"So, they'd say three veg? Maybe like a carrot and two Brussels sprouts, or maybe a Cucumber or an aubergine even. I guess it depends on how honest they're feeling"

Golden nuggets of conversation today in our ND house...

Son, wants to draw worry but struggling with ideas. We talk through some imagery but he can't 'see' it. Asks me to do a rough sketch to help. He looks at my attempt before delivering his verdict.

" It looks like an angry dinosaur" 😂

———

Daughter, " Thank you for my (Aloe Vera) plant. I'm going to call her Veronica. I know she can be Vera for short but I feel she needs a more substantial name with some gravitas. "

———

"Hot dogs are truly disgusting. The taste, the smell, the texture. They attack your senses. I shun them. They belong in the house of shun."
"Who else lives in the house of shun?"
"Certain celebrities who give damagingly inaccurate portrayals of autistic women. They belong in the basement deep in the dungeon of the house of shun…
With the Tories."

———

I hate small flies, like fruit flies.
They attack me and scare me.

I really doubt that its attacking you love. It just happens to be near you.

Oh really? Well why is it trying to invade me (sticking tissues in ears) by getting in my hair? I'm defending myself. It's not going in my ears.

Maybe it was lost?

That's about as convincing as Putin's rationale.
The fly is simply invading me. It is inexcusable. It is the Putin of flies.

The woman in the mirror

I sit here on the floor. Waiting. Again.

I swallow down my frustration with a chaser of saccharine sweet reassurances to smooth the waters. And wait it out. The meltdown will pass. In time.

It strikes me suddenly that now and for the past two years, I have been 'on hold.'

Me, this demi woman I've become, is on hold. And during this time, I have lost who I was and am yet to discover who I will be.

I see the woman in the mirror, and don't recognise her as me. I don't identify with the image staring back. She looks so old and tired. Extra weight on waist and thighs, unwashed hair still dragged up in a 'messy bun' in a vague attempt to disguise the lockdown home haircut. Chipped nail polish on her toes, and unshaven legs.

Today he bought me some new clothes. In a larger size. For comfort. And a dress. He was so proud and happy.

His excitement as he handed me the bag was tangible...as though the items contained by this miraculous but unassuming parcel, had the power to bring back his wife.

I slipped into the trousers, trying to look and sound pleased. They were nice enough. Classic...blue, functional. Good.

And a dress. A dress that fitted perfectly but which made me feel even more of an imposter. Like a small child playing dress up, in an overly glamorous outfit. Barefoot. Naked face. He was thrilled. Made his advances. But I couldn't respond, not because I don't love him. But because I don't feel it. Authentic. Loveable.

I'm not enough for this dress. This semi-woman I've become. It looks wrong on her. The woman in the mirror.

The illness so far reaching, its tendrils clawing beyond the damage they inflict on my children and into the heart of us. The days spent in crisis, the surviving one minute at a time. Holding them, guiding them. Fending off demons.

There is no place for self-grooming in that kind of life. So, my colour has gone. I'm a black and white wife.

When you spend months just trying to make it to bedtime without one of other of your beloved children sharing that they want to die.

And you must not cry.

You stay afloat by ignoring the woman in the mirror.

And then there's the trauma. When your child is so traumatised by their school (where you once worked. In another life) that the triggers are everywhere. So, you throw out your work clothes, the make-up you wore, the perfume, the shoes in a heap on the floor.

All had to go. Stripped away for the trauma they cause. Your child cannot bear to see any part of the woman you were, because in their head, she was complicit in their distress. It's a mess. It's like someone has strewn tiny landmines throughout your home. They could blast at any moment. Stay alert. Heightened vigilance and a dash of adrenalin...your staple diet. So, you throw out that old part of your identity. Bin bag for your autonomy.

The smiling, competent professional, a ghost. She's gone. You gave her up willingly, was necessity. You needed to be, there. When they needed you most?

So, you find yourself here. Trying to carve a new path. Taking heart from the tiny tangible steps towards a brighter day…and you stay at home. Lockdown persists for you. And the woman in the mirror.

Sometimes you dream, it sustains you to believe that it won't always be this way. You feel self-indulgent and vain so you will not complain. Instead reading and searching, networking and learning. New ways to connect to help and protect, nurture their self-respect. And all along you sing to their song help them find their own strong.

And one day, when they have found their way. Their zest, their path…you might laugh again. And wear makeup and shoes.

You might feel like you.

And not the woman in the mirror.

Acceptance

I read another post today
In a forum for parents supporting their children with MH.
Frustration, sadness, futility there in black and white.
Seeking solace and comfort.
Again.
So much pain.
But another word leapt out at me... acceptance.

I've carried it around with me since.
That word.
Trying to work out
What it means for me,
And could mean for us.

Is acceptance giving up?
Is it losing hope?
Acceptance feels synonymous with defeat.
But what if it isn't?

What if acceptance could set us free?
What if acceptance means we can acknowledge that where we are is damned hard.
And dark.
But instead of fighting it, we accept,
That for now, this is how it is.

What then?

Could we begin to embrace the tiny chinks of light?
What if, by accepting where we are now
We disempower the grief we are feeling,
For the loss of who we were,
the path we once saw?
And it dims,
just a little.

Enough
Just enough
for us to celebrate the small victories in where we are
What if it allows us to feel gratitude for the wonders that mean so much more now than in our previous lives.

Birdsong
An embrace
The flicker of a smile
The beauty of a crisp winter morning
The froth on our coffee...
And we begin to know a different kind of meaningful.

And by letting go of longing
We find peace with the present.

Knowing all the while

That acceptance is not giving up.

It is standing beside our children

Not pushing them forward

Or weeping for what once was.

But accepting that where we are now

Has a beauty all its own.

Messy

Chaotic

Or silent

and still

It is our present,

And it is real.

Steps

My mother, with whom I rarely speak; said yesterday to remember this is a journey. It's not your destination or theirs.

It's true.

But there are days when the scenery is bleak and the exhaustion is too much.

The futility of the situation... moving forward only to move back, can feel overwhelming. Often not moving at all.

It is a journey, but the only kind I know of where you have to believe and keep believing things can change, whilst often sitting still.

For a long…

Time.

Inertia.

Futility.

They are not travelling companions.

They are the diverted buses

The cancelled trains.

The closed motorways.

It is a journey.

Often lonely.

Often dark.

Often stationary.

How can we travel whilst going nowhere?

The frustration

So raw

Such fire

As we watch others hop on their train

Off for a carefree day

By the coast

With family or friends

Enjoying the simple pleasures

Of travel

Company Music

Our train sits in the platform

Unoccupied

Another delay announced

Then a cancellation

Not today

It wasn't meant to be

And we must allow ourselves to feel sadness and disappointment

We are human after all.

But acceptance and hope

Our new tour guides.

Introduced to us by others who travel this way.

Showing us that even the tiniest change, imperceptible to others

Is a step.

Is a hope.

Is movement.

This is not a journey of trains

Planes or

Cars

Miles covered at great speed.

No.

There is no ETA

This is a journey of steps.

Often small.

It could be a smile

A word

A hug

A meal.

It counts.

If today feels static,

Stagnant, still

If it's is all there is today...

It is a step.

So, whilst others enjoy the scenery

Whizzing past their windows

Ours is a longer journey

A slower journey

A different journey

And when we accept our pace

Learn to look for and celebrate our unique landmarks

We can see it's a journey none the less

And every day

Although tiny

And sometimes backwards

There will be steps.

Xx

Making Chilli

There are days when you try to distract yourself (by making chilli, then maybe soup,) from the gut-wrenching pain of hearing your child, on call to the psychiatrist calmly stating that they want to kill themselves because they are lonely and sad, but don't feel brave enough. Going on to say that in those times mum reminds them of some things to feel grateful/happy for. Like their loyal, funny little dog. And sometimes it works. And sometimes it doesn't.

To an extent, when you hear these words over 2-3 years, you almost become a little desensitised in order to carry on. But there are days, maybe today because you heard them say it aloud talking to someone else, when hearing those words just simply crushes you.

Ghosts

Yesterday I walked among the ghosts, the ghosts of who we were.

The sun shining down as if it knew, adding vibrance to the familiar cobbled streets. Exotic aromas drifting between the market stalls, conjuring images of sun-kissed beaches. Smiling, maskless faces, revelling in the closeness of friends. Laughter, voices, music and they drink in the freedom. Their laughter mocking our secular existence. What we are now. No roadmap for us, no date set by Boris for our freedom.

The rhythmic trundle of scooter wheels breaks through my melancholy ponderings as a smiling, red cheeked boy weaves among the crowds until brought to an abrupt stop by a stern looking market officer.

"No scooting in here please mate"

Such a mundane, simple phrase and yet those words make my heart contract and my breath catch in my throat. I see the ghosts of the people we used to be, the life we lived then.

That was him, me, us. Only two short summers ago. This was our place, our pace. Me and my smiling, red cheeked boy.

My smiling, red cheeked boy. Face bronzed from long, hot days in the sun. Hours of running, jumping, climbing, chatting, scooting. Always on the go!

The clatter of the scooter wheels across the cobbles as he waves at the stall holders, they wave back and smile. He looks over his shoulder, laughing that I can't keep up. Always ahead- leading the way. Knowing his way.

And the sun shines. The smiling maskless people are revelling in the closeness of friends, laughter, voices, music, drinking in the freedom.

I walk among them. Intentionally invisible in my glasses and mask. Avoiding the well-intentioned enquiries...

"How is your son? "

I cannot face the expected response...

"He's fine thank you"

He sits alone you see. In a darkened room seeking solace from the company of his gaming friends. His tribe who also walk this walk and know this pain.

He waits at home. Imprisoned by his inner demons.

He used to come here and scoot, my smiling, red cheeked boy. When the demons were quieter. Before they became so powerful and loud that this warrior mama knows not how to silence them...though I will never stop trying...

So, I walk among the ghosts.

My heart contracts, and my breath catches in my throat.

And I complete my mission.

I buy him some fudge. From his favourite haunt where once he laughed and joked and chatted... my smiling, red cheeked boy.

I take the fudge home to his darkened room.

As he unwraps it, he smiles, and for a moment the demons are quiet.

He tastes the sugary treat and remembers, my smiling, red cheeked boy remembers and he tastes freedom.

Yesterday I walked among the ghosts. My heart contracted; my breath caught in my throat...but I learned a valuable truth.

Demons don't like fudge.

Last night, just for a while the demons were quiet and he emerged from the darkened room. He came downstairs. He hugged the dogs, he played tennis in the garden and jumped and ran and laughed in the sun...my darling boy

He laughed in the sun

My smiling, red cheeked boy.

The moving staircase

An early start
(After a late night)
For some quiet, and coffee.
Time for me.
Before…
Morning routines,
green tea with honey and a kiss for one,
For the other
Juggling, singing,
eye spy on the duvet cover
Cereal in bed
And meds.

Transitions take time
No short cuts or straight lines
Bed to bathroom
With a joke, or a song
To move things along
One in the shower
(After an hour)
The other is dressed
And trying her best
Make up
Jeans
She means business today.

We've planned a trip out
Just she and I
Some time away from the circus
Just us,
To be.
Free.

One is ready
Nerves a little unsteady
But dressed and bag packed
Has a drink and a snack

The other in towels
On the bed
Holding their head
Curled into a ball
Looking so small.
And it all comes undone

With the words:
'Don't go mum
I need you!
I'm scared!
I can't do this alone
Please just stay home'

Then despite knowing it's futile
I try for a while
To reason, reassure
To talk strategies
Techniques
But anxiety peaks
Can't talk anymore

On the floor
One on the floor
The other ready by the door.

And in that moment
I miss
Our life before all of this,
Heartbreak.
Before anxiety ruled
And our world
became
small.

The fear becomes anger
The panic now fight
Fewer words
For a while
(Dodging the missiles)
Think on my feet

Whose needs I can meet,
First

The storm begins to subside.

Now she's not here by my side
As we planned
Instead, she sits on her bed
Reluctantly thinking
what could we do instead?

She heard all their tears
has felt the same panic,
The terror so manic
 Knows the dread,
But today
they feel it instead

So, despite best laid plans
The make-up,
The clothes,
She knows.
When their fear is so loud
A fear like her own
Plans have to change
You can't be alone.
Or even with dad

Because although it feels sad
Sometimes,
In the darkest moments
Only
Mum
Will do.

And a fragile calm is restored
Once they know
We
Won't
go.

They are now settled and eating
A cooked breakfast to munch through
Knowing that today they don't have to fight their demons
Without me too.

And, striking with the iron now cold
I don't chastise or scold them
Instead talking of small steps
We can take next
Towards time apart
When their heart
Feels
Stronger

Then up the stairs,
My heart heavy
And full
of unshed tears

God it's been years!
How much more can we bear?
Then
She's there.

She's smiling
Arms open
She holds me and I her
No words, I need
To follow her lead.
Despite her foiled plans
For our day out together

She knows
It won't be this way forever
And whilst her wings are clipped by
Circumstance
She's learned to dance to another tune.

She scoffs at my apology
And she shares her analogy
 And just wow!

"You see it's like how,

There are moving staircases

In a magical castle.

You step on going one way

But it moves

changes direction

Like today.

And as the staircase twists

And turns

You learn,

To embrace

the new place where you find yourself

(Other dreams on the shelf

For another

Day.)

So, you see

Mum it's ok!

We can still just

go for a walk

We can still talk.

That's where the staircase took us today. "

My heart bursts

Jaw on the floor

In total awe
Of the wisdom she holds
Her words still unfold.

"We'll take joy
In the small things
Today
The ones others don't see,
Lolloping dogs
Autumn leaves
Dewy cobwebs
You
and me.

It won't always be this way
Our plans can wait
For another day"

So, we hug
Then find boots
We don't need the car
Not going far
Today

And her wise words
Resound
Her thoughts so profound

"This is not our forever,

But, we ride the moving staircase,

Because..

We're all in this together"

♥ ♥ ♥

Anecdotes from Neurodivergent family life…

I honestly don't care what colour the balloon weights are. I have no preference, pink or blue would've been fine. Colours have no gender dad. It's not like blue has a cock.

———

I like the Jekyll and Hyde analogy. The OCD is an illness, it turns them into Mr Hyde who is violent and cruel and destructive.
Dr Jekyll loathes it and wants to find a way to contain that beast. Dr Jekyll is the hero.

———

I needed to wash your make up brushes as a distraction to calm me. It didn't work because it smelled like goat!

———

I'm going to fall asleep dreaming (well, imagining and wishing whilst asleep which I guess is the same thing) of a Utopian community based in a rural English village, occupied by leftists.

———

At this point in time, I have no desire to become an adult. I shall not partake in adulthood. I'm going to start sleeping with the window wide open, hell I might sleep outside so I can welcome Peter Pan and he can whizz me off to Neverland.

———

"I'm sorry that things are so tough right now and that it limits what we can do"

" Are you kidding me? I have time now to explore and research, religion, sexuality, gender, fashion...I'm learning about myself in a way I couldn't before. And, I can just read for pleasure!"

In the dark

In the dark

Alone

Quiet

I can eat

Drink

Think

In the dark

Breathe

In the dark

Clock ticks

Counting hours

Go to bed

You should go to bed

Yet I stay here

In the dark

Breathe

In the dark

Autonomy

For just a while

I smile

At the tv

One episode rolls into another...

In the dark

Breathe

In the dark
I pause
I rest in the solitude
Process the day
Its ok to cry
In the dark

Breathe

In the dark
Free to recall
It all
The carefree chaos
That once filled these rooms
I hear the laughter
In the dark

Breathe

In the dark
I regroup
I restore
Build my strength up
Once more,
In the dark

Breathe

In the dark

I plan for tomorrow

Make a plan

Can the sorrow

In the dark

Breathe

In the dark

I give in

Weary body

Needs rest

Just can't fight

Sleep

In the dark

Breathe

In the dark

Tv playing

I nod and dream of days

I won't need to remind myself

To…

Breathe…

In the dark,

I visit days that were,

And pray

For days to come

When we'll laugh
Together
In the sun
In the sun
And I won't need to sit alone
In the dark…

The glue

Every so often
It hits me
The futility
The enormity
Of what we are facing
Every single day

Claustrophobia
Clenches at my throat
My heart pounds
Races
But there's no finish line in sight.

No respite
From the desperation
I feel as we face
The start of another year
Still
Here.

A lockdown so long
Can't bear to be caged
Watching with envy
The birds
In the garden...

Flying away.
Away.

In that moment
The plates come crashing down
Home
Finance
Fragile hearts
Broken apart

For a moment.

Then despite the clenching in my throat
My heart pounding from my chest
I pick up the plates
There is no rest for me
The glue.

Hold it together

It won't be forever
I tell myself
And I try to keep sight of how far we have come
When the future feels bleak
And black.

Don't look back.
Keep looking ahead
Get out of bed
Make the coffee
Get the meds
And breathe.

I can't
I won't
leave
So sometimes
All I can do

Is breathe.
And count the smiles
The triumphs
However small

They are real.
They are ours
They are true.

And I look at you.
The warrior ones
Fighting an invisible fight
I cannot protect you from
This enemy...

But I see

You.

Everything else falls away

Because I see

You.

However huge this feels for me.

I will not give up.

Until

You

Are

Free.

So, I swallow the fear

Though it screams

in my ears

And dance to the beat

of my racing heart

I cannot fall apart.

A beginning

Today was a beginning,
Stepping out hand in hand
We found ourselves, you and I.
Ourselves and each other.

Sipping coffee, river breeze,
Crunchy, golden leaves beneath us
and clear blue skies above.
My love.

Our world became a little larger,
Brighter
Hope igniting, exciting. Freedom.
And the sun, the wind, the rain.
Sweet rain again.

For so long gripped by this covid-esque lockdown.
Shutdown.
Down.
Behind closed doors,
hearts and souls kept captive

As the insidious gaoler
Tightened its grip.

On them
And us.

Our family made puppets dancing to the tune of their OCD, anxiety.
No autonomy.
Holding back the walls as they closed in around us.

Plans cancelled, staying home, outings a remnant of our past selves.
Looking inward, finding with creativity we could find ways to fill our days.
But longing all the while for liberation.

You my love, making my heart swell.
Through the long, dark days, this illness haze, you standing tall.
Together finding ways to climb the wall.

A little walk, when we could.
To the woods.
Long enough to fill our lungs with
Less insipid air.
Wind in your mass of curly hair.
Untamed and wild,
then home.

Home, a fortress
And a battleground,
the war it rumbles on.
You stay home, as I stay home...to fortify and keep them strong.

Your room a refuge,
Filled with all things calming, soothing.
Feel good films, and dancing gear,
Make up art, well it's a start
For when we can go out.

And then a change in circumstance
We seize the chance
Reassure them, they are ready
Dad is there
To keep them steady, for a while.

We smile,
and although you're feeling rushed
Your hair yet to be brushed,
We go.
Door closes, world opens.

Wheels turning, as our yearning
Grows.
Nearly there
Wind in hair

Hand in hand
Outside we stand.

The wider world is not that far
By car

Two hours. Two whole hours
Of walking, talking
Smelling, tasting autumn.
Neither one of us can stop smiling.
Walking through the ancient park
down to the river.

And all at once we find ourselves
In the midst of smiling faces, proud parents,
Photos and celebrations.
Young people in graduation gowns,
Beginning their stories as their loved ones look on.

The beautiful, historic buildings tower over us. Stoic and strong.
Here starts your song.
Here starts your song.

Your face lights up, not just with the autumn sun
but with good things to come.
Your wings clipped by circumstance
For so long

Are beginning to spread

Free from the dread

For a while.

Here, in this place

We have the space

to dream,

to hope,

to plan

And away from the confines

We both know you can.

We both know you can.

Fortified by our journey

We start the road back.

They're waiting, we know

For them time's passing is slow

And we are needed again

But we're

Changed by this respite

A break from the long fight

Rested, connected

Souls nourished and fed

We can weather the dread

The world is not so small,

We can see now over the wall.
Over the wall.

So, we head home

We do so with smiles
Although gone but a while
the impact was profound

We walked on new ground and found
Aspiration
breaking free from frustration...

Now dogs bark, car parked
Showers demanded by the puppeteer
They're just relieved we're here
We're home. Now they can relax.
I am back.

And as we step into the circus once more
We know there'll be more, than this.
There will be more for you, than this.

Today was a beginning
Stepping out hand in hand

We found ourselves, you and I

Ourselves and each other

Daughter and mother

Singing in the car

I close the car door. Reach for my seat belt and turn the key.
Just me.
Alone.
With my music.
I press the button on the display
Selecting a song that will fit how I'm feeling, what's in my heart, just now.

"Believe"

A ballad, a love song, a power anthem...
The opening bars wash over me and suddenly I can...
Breathe.

Three men whom I'll never meet,
Singing songs that speak of my innermost self,
 As though the words were written for me,
For this story.
There are simply some songs that speak to my soul.
That ignite me,
And nourish my weary heart.
And they must be played loud,
So very loud,
And I sing with all the strength I have.
The windows rattle as though

A battle is in full flow,

But no,

It's just me singing,

Roaring my defiance to the world.

From the safety of my car,

Contained but not restrained.

The lyrics tell of strength,

Of love,

And of giants.

I drive the long route to make the moment last,

Finish my song.

Throat almost hoarse.

But refreshed.

Uplifted.

I park the car.

Turn the key.

Back to being Me.

But as I step outside,

I'm a little less small.

My heart pounding in my chest,

Creates a rhythmic beat.

As though the song, an incantation,

Has revived me,

Renewed me.

And whilst I am surely no giant,

My woes do feel slightly smaller,

As if the music,

The song,

Changed me,

Charged me...

A giant?

No.

But ready to be strong.

Friends with a twist

The last few years have taught me a great deal about friendship and connection.
It has taught me that the length of time you have known someone has no bearing on the deep connection you can share through common lived experience or through genuine love and acceptance.
Because this life we lead is not the norm,
and those that would join us on this journey are a special few.

You thought you knew?

But our challenges are a world apart. So, if you are a friend in this strange reality, the chances are you either share our story or, you are a rare breed of human, able to offer support and kindness without judgement or demand.
You may not 'get it'
but you'll still hold a hand.
Because this life we lead is not the norm.

Kind of a mess.

A journey, a storm.

Think ... a comedy that is so far-fetched that it's not quite believable, or funny... or a drama so gritty and raw you can't

look and have to turn over,
or a movie with unassuming heroes achieving impossible feats.
It's a thriller,
edge of your seat,
adrenalin rushing and just when you think you've reached the happy ending...
have it all figured out...
there's a twist!
Always a twist.
And it's at those times, in those moments I have experienced true friendship and loss.

Because this ride is just too rough for some.
Overcome by the intensity,
too gritty,
Unrelentingly raw.
Some just draw,
A line.

And that's fine,
You'll find no malice or judgement.
You just weren't meant
To be My friend.

By losing those who found it too much to stay
I found friends,
allies, comrades

In alternative ways.

Are you the friend ...
The one I called from the bathroom floor?
The lock in pieces
The door...
broken
And me, desperate to remove the catch
But couldn't figure it out, going out of my mind
You were calm, practical and kind.
Helped me find, a way to fix it. So that it was safe.
Could not be locked
From the inside.
Didn't have to pretend or hide
My tears.
From you.
You knew what had happened
Could happen again.
But no longer alone,
You helped figure it out,
Somehow felt you bedside me
From the end of the phone.

Are you the friend...
The one who needed to take a break?
To step back
It was all just too much

And we lost touch
for a while.
But a thread still remained
And it drew us close
When the time was right.
Now, you fight
The voice in my head
When it says I just can't,
I can't take any more,
And I call in a mess
From my kitchen floor.

Are you the friend...
The one I'd not seen in years?
Then we found common truths
We had walked a shared path
And through text chats and phone calls,
We share distant tears.

Are you the friend...
Whose face I've never seen?
But you know just how I feel
You too live this life
Your compassion so real.
Connection online
With so many others
Fighting demons

Tending wounds
Not experts
Just mothers.

Are you the friend…
Who lives so far away?
We once worked together
(In another life)
And laughed
And had fun.
Before all this had begun.
But you're there,
And you'll listen
give validation, hold space.
As I wipe away tears
And paint on a new face.

Are you the friend…
Who needed me too?
And using my own experience
I guided you through?

And yet, there are times when I'm lonely
Although not alone.
Long distance connection
Barely leaving home.

Yes the last few years has taught me a lot about connection, and friendship. I've learned to treasure those who walk beside me or just behind in case I fall.

I've learned to pick up the phone, text and call, you.

The ones who remain, and those I'm still meeting,
Rushed conversations,
Connections are fleeting.
And through this strange TV guide that's my life
With heart break as mother
Imposter as wife
You watch it all with me,
Even messy and raw
You don't just turn over,
you don't just ignore.
I weather the plot twists that happen each day
Knowing you have my back

And you chose to stay. 🩶

Anecdotes from Neurodivergent family life…

If you put a peach under the tap it splashes you, mum".
"Yes, it's a hard object."
"I thought only spoons did that."
"Any hard object."
"Makes no sense…Peaches are soft"

———

It sounds as though you are managing the situation amazingly and know your child so well. I can't really suggest anything more psychologically. But do make sure you are supported; it is very intense caring for a child with mental illness.
No shit Sherlock.

———

Daughter (taking her lunch break from A Level History and having a dog cuddle) "I have been educating the dogs mum. They now respond to the word feminist, they understand it and they are clear that we eat, but do not become Tories. No child of mine shall be a Tory."

———

Mother's Day made by my wonderful daughter and her unique perspective and observations:

1. Mum, this is what motherhood has done, you've been 'doing lines' of toast crumbs

2. Whilst on dog walk, explaining the sea to her dog.
" So, it's a large body of water, it may look flat at times but you cannot just run over it. Well unless you're Jesus"

3. I hate the Russian dictator.
He needs to be humiliated and ridiculed, painfully. Chopping off his penis, and surgically sticking it to his forehead should do it. Rebrand him as a 'Puticorn'

4. Still on dog walk as Police forensic van passes.
" I learned how you can tell the ethnic origin of a pubic hair"
" How?"
" At school. My dodgy teacher put a weird documentary on about catching offenders"
" I mean how can you tell?"
"Under a microscope the molecules look closer together or further apart depending on ethnic origin"

" Oh OK. I thought you meant by sight."

" No mother. Well unless they're Ginger, which would be unfortunate!"

Mummy come and lay beside me.

I'm sorry I was so angry before; I didn't mean the things I said to you.

You are trying your best and you are autistic too so it's even harder for you.

So, I think you are the best mum in the whole world.

(Strokes my hair)

Mummy lie down with me.

I'm sorry about before, I didn't mean it but the OCD made me so angry. But you are trying your best I know you are. And you're autistic too so it's even harder but you still try really hard to help me.

So, you must literally be the best mummy in the whole world.

(post meltdown cuddles ♥)

Listen to the professionals

Listen to the Professionals
We are taught
Accept their judgements,
Their opinions
Blindly
Because surely
They
Know
Best.

They have the training,
The certificates
The authority
To decide the fates of our children,
Our families.

Such power in the hands of a few
Who don't really know you,
Or your child.

Challenge them?
Be considered wild,
Rogue
'That mother'
The anxious one, thinks she knows best for her son (or

daughter)

No, she ought, to just accept what's been decided.

Fall in line.

Afterall, apparently our children are 'Fine' In school.

Only they're not.

At

All.

There have been so many who had they been inclined

To listen

To validate

Could have saved so much pain and hate

She now feels towards herself.

The SENDCo with the sickly smile

Stroking your arm

All the while muttering platitudes

And fairy-tales of a happy contented child,

Not the child you know and see.

"Mum you're very anxious, it could be you, not her you see"

Gaslighting becomes the norm

Parent blaming endemic,

Until you question yourself

Could they be right?

Each time it happens,

You lose a little more
Fight.

The Mental Health coordinator
With clip board
And paper work
Questioning and quizzing
Why is diagnosis so important?
What will it achieve?
You literally cannot believe
She said that.

How about identity? Self-compassion? Understanding?
Unmasking?
Recovery and mending
Her fragile heart?
The woman's condescending tone.
Announces that you are fighting this fight
Alone.

Schools point the finger
Of blame, disbelief.
Attendance figures, sanctions.
Just get them into class.
No matter the trauma
That will last.
And last.

But then,
(And when you felt all hope had gone)
Came the one you had waited for.
Who would listen, validate
Restore,
Your faith in 'professionals'

She asked questions
and stopped to hear the answers you gave!
She had ideas, support to offer
And, thanks to her
You felt you may actually save
Your child
More pain,
More despair.
Because one professional
Took a moment
To care.
And where there's one, there's another
A psychiatrist who listens!
Has a plan, knows they can
Help your child.

No longer considered wild,
Or rogue.
A team who see you,

For the mother you are.

Desperate for help,
Your child can't leave the car...
Or their home,
Or their bed.
They're stuck in a cycle,
Need safety
From the terrors
That dance in their heads.

This team see your truth
They have seen countless others,
Broken children,
Lost youth
And soul-destroyed mothers
Who keep going.

Knowing,
That with the right 'professionals'
There could just be a chance
To find the light, that's gone out in her eyes.
She might dance,
Again
One day.

But for now, it's enough

That these professionals

Have seen her,

Heard her,

Freed her

With diagnosis,

Support,

Empowering her to cope

They gave back her future

They gave back your

Hope.

Brain washing

You sat in the garden today
Took a break from the lesson
Overcome,
Overwhelmed.

And in the peace
Underneath the trees
It came to you

Memories
Assemblies
Warning speeches
Cautionary tales
Of exam fails

You had an epiphany in that moment
As you relived the lectures
And lessons
"These grades will stay with you forever
You will never shake them
But wear them always,
A dog collar of grades,
That will stay
With
You."

Failure means shame
Don't dare to blame
Mental health
It's
Your
Self.

Academic success
Doing your best
Is all that matters
Even if it shatters
Your
Heart.
Tears
You
Apart.

The memories you realise
Now you see with new eyes
Are what has caused such distress
All this mess
In your head.
They made you believe
That grades,
And school,
Are all
There is.

They spewed dread and fear
Made the real you
Disappear
They dismissed your distress
Thought that they knew best
Suck it up
Get in line
At school she's
Just
Fine.

But you were far from ok.
Those feelings have stayed.
And here in this space
With the sun on your face
The breeze in your hair
You went back there.

And now you see with such clarity
The power of words
Their opinions absurd
Damaging speeches
Self-esteem leeches
They had it so wrong
You believed for so long

And today you have seen
How hard it is to shake
The feelings of shame
And self-blame
How they make you doubt your worth
Your place on this earth.

A squirrel dashed by
Caught your eye
Brought you back from that place
Felt warmth on your face.
You watched him climb the tree
Haphazardly
And smiled
For a while.
Because with hindsight
You can now see.
It's not top scores
Or high grades
That get you through
It's knowing your heart
Making a start
Learning how to be you
Academic success

And what of the rest?
The courage to know

We all have to grow

Learn to try

And to trust

That you are enough

And there

Under the sun

You came to see

The greatest treasure

You hold is

Authenticity.

The faceless one

It started with clothes
And shoes,
Then make up, bags and photographs.
It took them from me.
The faceless one.
Forced me to shed my skin
The only way to save them,
Spare them,
more torment and distress.

Tangible objects that had been to 'that place,'
and could contaminate their safe space with the poison they
felt inside.
'They must all go'
the faceless one demanded.
And I complied
Couldn't hide
From it.

The day they touched a keepsake box
Stashed on a high shelf
Until they found it
Accidentally.
The colour had drained from their skin
Panic begins to surge.

Triggered tears and self-harm
Fight or flight in full flow
The punches thrown
My way.
As the faceless one smiled.
It rewrote our past,
the faceless one.
Smearing pain and hurt
With its 'dirt'
Until they could no longer separate
The happy times
From the pain
A stain...on it all
From that school.

They cannot say the name
See a picture,
drive nearby or
Breathe the air
Says the faceless one.
And they believed its lies
As they cried.

And as the poison grew
So did its hold on you
Plagued by ghosts
Memories of people

Places,

Voices,

Faces,

Nightmares

Left them shaking

As the faceless one was making

Itself at home.

It took away photos

Toys, games and books

They just couldn't look

At those things

They had owned

At that time.

And the faceless one

Placed tiny landmines (called triggers)

Throughout our home

Smells, objects and sounds

Ready to detonate

Their angst

Their hate

We try to avoid them

As best we can

But the faceless one is wily and clever

We never know

Where

They

Are.

The Christmas star

The photo of grandad, they had

Such fun with him.

The decorations we had had for years

Our family keepsakes

Now trigger their tears.

'Throw it all out'

The faceless one insists

As they cry

to erase their childhood

They would if they could.

'Those years are all bad'

The faceless one says

Won't let them see

There were happier days.

And now it shouts ever louder

The faceless one

Because they have begun

Their journey.

Smiling

Doctors (are they knights?)
Ready to help them fight,
To teach them the ways
They can say..
no more.
To find chinks in its armour
The faceless one
Yes this fight has begun.

But this is more a war,
The Drs say.
Will take months, maybe years
It will be here
to stay
For now

I will outwit it, I vow
If I can figure out how
The faceless one
Works,
where it lurks
This enigma
This faceless one has a name
the Drs say
PTSD

You see

It's not reserved for soldiers

Not created in a day.

But by many,

This way.

Loneliness

Isolation

Bullying

humiliation

A broken heart

That's where it started

The faceless one

And as time went by its tendrils grew

And it just knew

How to hurt them, haunt them,

Cause fear and pain

Again

And

Again.

But the Drs can see it

The faceless one

They know its games

They shared its name,
with them and us.

And now they know, they aren't alone
On this journey
Their band of knights
(In white coats) are teaching
And we're learning.
How to live beside it.

We'll play it at its own game
Think outside the box
And pack away the landmines

The ones we can... find.

Help them to challenge it
When they're feeling stronger
Pack away the pictures,
Keepsakes, treasures
Until the day they're landmines
no longer.

Because there will be a day
Though not a near tomorrow
When they will break free
From its lies,

its pain,

its sorrow...

The faceless one.

Happy Mother's Day

A hug,
A smile (masking her anxiety about events to come tomorrow)
Normal morning routines (must be observed, for comfort and to feel safe)
A beautiful card,
With pop up daffodils (my favourite flowers)
And a personal verse
Of love and thanks from my daughter (the wise one)
Melts my heart
A bracing, soul soothing walk in the fresh air
Dogs bounding gleefully through wet grass.
Comical observations on life and the world,
Through her eyes.
My heart smiles.

Home
Youngest sobbing.
Full of angst and pain.
Searching online:
Most efficient ways to kill yourself.

My heart braces itself.

Husband has tried
In vain to console them.

He retreats to make tea,
To fortify me as I step up.

I offer comfort and support,
From a distance (they want space)
The dog senses need and offers a squeaky dinosaur.
To no avail.

They live an online life (OCD demands they stay inside)
Friendships made and broken, through a screen.
So intense.
They are the only 'friends' they have.
A game ban or confrontation
Feels catastrophic
And brings waves of loneliness
And despair.
Right now, they're drowning.

Discreetly offer drink and snacks,
A little life buoy of a momentary connection,
And back away.

The comforting aroma of
Roast lunch
Wafts through the house
And reaches them.

They put down the headset

And hug the dog

Drawing comfort from the musty scent of wet grass on fur.

Equilibrium restored for now.

They return to gaming

And chat with a companion from the other side of the globe.

Whilst driving a car around a virtual city.

From a chair.

In the corner of the sitting room...

Lunch shared,

Daughter joins us for gifts and hugs.

This too is a gift (more precious than any other)

She often prefers the solitude and safety of her room.

Surrounded by her books and plants.

We eat.

We smile.

We dare to make plans. Together.

Youngest waves from the sitting room.

I smile inside.

These moments of connection,
They are my everything.
I know they are few, and rare,
So, I hold them tightly
(Wish that they may stay)

And I thank them,
My family,

For my Happy Mother's Day ♥

Through my eyes

On days like these,
I wish you saw through my eyes.
Walked my walk.
Felt my heart pound in my chest.
So loud it makes me breathless.

With fear
With sadness
With pride
Small shards of joy inside
Pounding the unrelenting rhythm of my day.
Could you see things this way?

You see:
I stayed up too late.
You couldn't wait, while I did a 2-hour bedtime routine.
You were tired and ready for bed.
But, instead, I stayed up.
For some quiet.
For some quiet.

The leaning tower of laundry.
Piled, high and hoping it'll be sorted and put away before it topples.
Again.

Your pants draw empty.

3 packets of butter open simultaneously.

3 half used jars of gravy granules in the cupboard

(you line them up as a visual reminder of my incompetence as a home maker)

The ancient treasures on the top shelf of the fridge…

pasta sauce, mustard and what once was yoghurt.

The lopsided rotary dryer in the garden..

rained on washing…

wasn't brought in before the downpour.

2 days ago.

It leans at a jaunty angle.

Precariously close to the muddy 'lawn'

Down to 1 loo roll.

Bin needs emptying.

3 dinners prepared,

all 3 rejected in favour of porridge

(which boiled over in the microwave)

because that's just how it is.

"The microwave is sticky - just saying"

The microwave is sticky.

NONE OF IT MATTERS!

Don't you see?

Those things are the balls I dropped whilst juggling many others.
Being a mother.

I'm not wearing makeup.
I didn't brush my hair.
Or shower.
Or shower.
No shower of affection for you.
You see a wife too tired for your amorous attempts.
But a cuddle won't do.
Not for you.

And our children...

The mask they wear, their winning act.
They smile for you,
knowing all too well that you aren't ready for them to bare their souls.

You can't fix them, mend them, bend them.
So, they smile.
You're still in love with the them they once were,
and with the dreams those children had to pursue.
With you.

You wince at their flapping or clapping.
Their questions and talk.
Their knowledge of tech or of flowers and birds.
To you seems absurd.

You can't walk their walk.

You don't see them shrink away from you a little more, with each thoughtless comment,
Another lock on the door of their hearts.
Another part they can't share.
They don't dare.

You won't celebrate their chatter, their
Curiosity or zest.

You
Apologise for them.
Infront of them.
Your children.

And they hear you. They hear you.

You see the flooded bathroom floor
The broken door
Watermarks on the ceiling
Punch that sent me reeling.

As the hurt bubbled over...

But not the tender apology or the courage to get out of the shower.
 Once the storm passed.

You hear the comments, reprimands..
demands.
The sharp tongue.
The fury, and fight.
You can't do anything right'
You can't see that the hurt and anger is not about you.
When the words fly your way..
Could you patiently stay?

You can't let it go and smile as I do (sometimes through gritted teeth)
knowing that the rage is simply spicy sadness.
Needing kindness.
Not self-indulgence.
So, you hide away to lick your wounds.
And I make another 3 dinners.
Make sure the kids are drinking (they forget)
And email school.

And make sure the right seamless pjs are clean and dry.
 And email school.

And email CAMHS.

And speak to the psychiatrist.

And sidestep a meltdown…
singing xmas songs outside the bathroom door whilst impersonating a dog.
Whatever raises a smile.
For a while.
And call the tutor.
And fill out another form
Another list in black and white of all the ways that mental health impacts our child.
And our family.

And feed the dogs.

And reassure that red skin doesn't make her any less beautiful.
And order skin care and pamper goods.
We're not out of the woods..

And support through flashbacks.
Distraction hacks.
And buy textbooks on amazon.

And pay the bills on the banking app.
And call CAMHS.
And email school.

Again.

Whilst you are licking your wounds.
You miss so much.
A gentle touch.
A smile.
A laugh.

She shares a meme
They tell you of a funny dream
A small victory
Over OCD
Her knowledge of...
Paganism
Herbalism
Skincare
Homewares
Armchairs
Politics
American west
Pretty retro vests...

But you miss it.

Their humour
The jokes
Cheeky smile once in a while.

On days like these

I wish you could see through my eyes

See past the sadness

And busy madness

You miss so much

When you're out of touch

And you would see

If you were me

Yes, neurodiverse

And my universe.

Monday morning

Why are Monday mornings so damned hard?
We don't go anywhere.
Do anything,
See anyone.
No traffic jams
No morning radio in the car
Waving them off,
Turning on my music and singing.

No.
No singing for me.
"PJ's at 10am on a Monday? Bliss!"
(The foolish ones would say)
And I watch them from my window.
With envy clawing at my throat.
Feeling I will choke.
Masking from the get go.
Can't ever let it show
Or they will implode.

My freedom
Sense of self
Appearance
Independence.

Gone.

Along with the singing.

So here I am, stuck.

" What luck! I'd love not to have school runs!"

Like living in a dystopian novel

The all seeing, all hearing ruler

"Mental illness"

Controls your every move,

And by default, mine.

Get in line!

What I wear,

When I speak and with whom,

So, forgive me

If I don't feel lucky.

On a Monday morning,

Still not dressed

Stuck,

In this room.

A glimpse of you

This week has been surreal

It feels precarious,

risky, dangerous

To name,

to own,

to feel

Hope.

But my heart doesn't listen,

And somewhere deep inside my chest

It smiles.

All the while wary,

Knowing that the darkness can return

As suddenly as a summer storm.

And as though in retaliation

Or defiance

I list,

I voice, I name.

Because I have seen glimpses of you again, my love.

I saw it in your smile as we flipped pancakes together

In a flour covered kitchen

(way past bedtime.)

You defied your OCD,
Stepped away from your PC,
And we laughed, mixed and whisked.
You danced your comical moves.
I caught a glimpse of you...

I saw it as you emerged from the shower,
Triumphant!
Been in there minutes, not an hour.
Compulsions,
rituals,
enslaved you for so long.
And flooded floors
And smashed in doors.
But you're breaking through
I caught a glimpse of you...

I saw it as you stepped beyond the safety of the kitchen,
You ventured onto the patio
And only those of you who know
The heartbreak of a housebound child
Will understand the fierce, the wild
Beating of my heart.
Because it was a start,
And you felt it too.
You stood blinking in the sunshine
I caught a glimpse of you.

I saw it as you talked online,
With your tutor in your class
At last,
Someone who understood
That with
Chatting, laughing,
Building trust,
You could.
You could, do science,
Make music,
Write a letter
So much better
Voicing what you want to learn, to do,
I caught a glimpse of you...

I saw it as you climbed into my bed
As dad drank his morning cup of tea,
You laid your head
Upon his shoulder.
In that moment,
You seemed wiser
Somehow older

This illness knows destruction well,
Had driven wedges,
Waged a war

Father and child
Separated Opposite sides
Of a bolted door.

But I saw it when you placed your arms
Around your father's neck
And laughed
And reminisced
Talked of bike rides that you missed
Together you made plans
Of things you'd like to try to do.
And although those plans could take some time,
I caught a glimpse of you.

Even as I write these words
I have to hold my nerve
There have been times
The darker days
Where Hope had seemed absurd.

But my love, at last, I caught a glimpse of you

And whilst I know that next week could be dark, or even in an hour
(OCD is so very strong,
Can pull you back into that shower)

Even if it does my love
It cannot take his week away

Your bravery,
courage and your humour,
These things are real,
Are true.

You defy the darkness

Step by step

I see a glimpse of you.

Dreams

I long for the day I stop holding my breath,
I don't need to be strong.
Or dread the morning
Or relish the silence of the night.

When I can just let the day unfold
No plans.

I long to...
Drive
anywhere, everywhere
Walk and walk in lanes and woods and fields
Talk with friends,
the ones who know me
See the sea
Feel the fresh air
Wind in my hair.

And breathe.

I long to see them smile
And laugh
And venture outside
This bubble.

I long to stop fighting
To lay down my sword
My armour
My shield
And rest in the knowledge that the war is won.

But it's just begun.
So weary and tired I summon my strength
Warrior mother?

No, not I. But I'll try.

We'll find hope
See the light
Where we can
Embrace change
Even small,
And climb that high wall...

A system to fight
As well as your demons

Breathing can wait

As can the wind and the fields and the sea.
And the friends who see me.
Help me on with my armour

To continue this fight

They'll lift up my shield and hand me my sword

And help me breathe under the weight of it all.

Under the weight of it all.

I'll stand tall.

(My dreams will sustain me

My day will come

They'll be standing beside me

Feel the wind

And the sun.)

Anecdotes from Neurodivergent family life…

There was not enough wine for today.

Conversation 1.
With daughter.

" I really think I've got a problem with picking at my skin."
"Yes love, it's come up a few times hasn't it. I saw something we could try; they're strips that you scratch at instead. We could try them out if you like?"
"Maybe"
" Anything's worth a try once don't you think?"
" No, not anything. Was Trump worth a try?"
" Well, no, but I wasn't speaking politically"
" Wake up Mum, everything's political"

Closely followed by conversation 2.
With younger sibling

"So, what even is a butt plug and what's it for mum? "
(Insert gentle conversation about where, with whom and how this term was heard, gentle explanation including the obligatory quiz from them on size and hygiene concerns)
" Would people do that? People do crazy stuff for pleasure"
(…and flounces off in very fluffy slippers and stripey pants, singing Dancing in the moonlight.)

Ok, so it took 3 hours. But you did it. You stepped back and gave them time and space. And now they're in the shower singing 'Bridge over troubled waters'
I'd say that's a win.

―――――

(On facing a fear- a panic attack trigger) "Tesco- I'm coming for you!"

―――――

Pleasant but ill-informed nurse in A and E:
I'm going to pop these wires on your chest, they will let me check your heart rate and go... ba boom ba boom ba boom ba...
Daughter:
I'm autistic, not 5, just do it.
(To self: fucktard)

―――――

Please don't interrupt me. I'm going on an imaginary Pokémon hunt in my head.

―――――

So, I know you will appreciate that to survive we must find humour in dark times.

―――――

While I was out taking daughter to dance, me virtually cheerleading and her anxiety managing the whole way but she did it! 😊 😊 😊, two men had knocked on the door at home.
They were Labour party Counsellors.

Son phoned in distress

"There's strangers at the door, dad is talking to them and they are not social distancing - they need to go away!" (Shouts through the ring doorbell app)

"Go away, you need to step back. Don't pretend you can't hear me. Move away now"

Line goes dead.

Two minutes later son phones again.
"It's ok they have gone. I told them to leave or I would egg them out of my window"

Daughter:
"Wow. They must have thought he was an extremist Conservative"

😆

The cancelled appointments

There is an aspect of parenting young people through their Mental health challenges that is rarely voiced.

So much talk of bubble baths and emotional self-care, but what of our bodies? No one shares that challenge, the direct impact on a carer's physical health? When you simply cannot put yourself,

first.

I'm not talking about being tired, or run down, that's par for the course, but rather vital hospital or Doctor's appointments that you simply cannot get to.

Because they

Need

You.

Today I'm due a cervical smear. In forty minutes in fact.

It is long overdue.

I was sent a reminder, and then another.

But whenever an appointment was booked (and believe me they're hard to get at all) something always happened that meant I just couldn't get there.

I can't just leave you see.

They
Need
Me.

So many of us in the same catch 22, trying to push through, or find a way. Will it work today?

We need to look after our health because we are the one person on the planet our children feel safe with.

We can't look after our health because we are the one person on the planet our children feel safe with.

People say ' prioritise!' Or ' put your own parachute on first!'
They have no clue,
What it means to be you.

The last cancellation because my darling daughter had a sudden attack of vertigo. Literally paralysed with fear only the day before. She needed safety and comfort...not heart-wrenching separation anxiety on top of an already spinning world.

The time before that my youngest was having a very low week. I don't mean a little bit sad.
I mean in need of close monitoring for self-harm and suicidal thoughts. In need of Co regulation,

Re assurance,
My presence.

I don't remember the time before, or the one before that.

But I've made it here today.
Just.
Navigated PDA delays
Patience through gritted teeth, had to keep stress underneath.
Any sense of urgency, rush or hurry
And my plan would fail.
Just too much worry
For them.

Just too much.

But today, I made it,
I was late,
But
I made it.

And I realise, lying on the couch, how appointments like these, have a way of making us stare our mortality in the face.

Hard to support them in coping with this short lapse in care, what will happen you wonder, when you just can't be there?

Today I had my test, and then the rest.

Irregular pulse and "You need an ECG "

But aware of their fragilities "I'm in a rush you see,

they weren't expecting I'd be gone this long"

So, I lay on the bed, trying hard to focus on the lyrics of a song,

To slow my racing heart,

 I feel it pounding in my chest.

As I watch the clock.

Tick

Tock

No results just yet, so another appointment I will somehow have to get to.

They hand me a card, and utter the same words we've all heard before

"Now dear, you must be sure, to rest."

"Any more symptoms and it's off to the hospital "

And although clearly well meaning,

She knows nothing,

at, all.

I bolt to the car; the drive isn't far.

Music goes on

(self-indulgently loud)

Sing out my fears

Then
Suddenly
holding back tears...

As I stop at the corner
And there stands a mother, laughing and smiling.
Her young son joyously splashing in a puddle.

Shrieks of delight
And the light
In his eyes.

I remember those moments
And wish I knew then
To store them away
As you just don't know when
The light
Might
Go out.

A shout, from the driver behind
I gather myself and continue the drive
Irregular heartbeat and all,
Still strong.
Still alive.

And I know that I,
Like so many mothers
Will continue to miss, be late for, or cancel appointments
Because we've other
Priorities.

I pull onto the drive, to their relief
They can breathe now I'm home.
No longer fighting their demons alone.
I won't mention the ECG
Or the next Doctor check...
They don't need to know
(And I haven't yet worked out how I'll actually go.)

To my appointment.

Meh

Today, as I sat sipping coffee
(In the next room so far enough to give them space, but close enough to hear)
I smiled.

I smiled as I heard them greet their online tutor (Relieved they had managed to engage)
And exchange a simple greeting.
Ordinarily their tutor would enquire...
"How are you?"
The response would invariably be...
"Pretty awful"
"Rubbish"
Or
" Not good"
Only last week we had a ray of sunshine when the answer was a...
"Meh"

But today, today was different,
Today was new.
The coffee tasted sweeter,
The sunlight, streaming through the kitchen window luminescent,
And the cheerful, tuneful birdsong sang a celebratory chorus.

Today they simply said…
" I'm pretty good actually, how about yourself?"

I pinched myself.
So many stormy months,
And the dark, wintery clouds of depression casting their shadows over every aspect,
Of their every
Day.

I will treasure that phrase
"I'm pretty good actually"

I'll store it away
And remember,
That it heralded
The beginning of spring.

Chips by the river

I wore lipstick that day
And I swept up my hair,
Hoping,
praying
to get her there.

All the while knowing that at any given moment, 'Rain' could stop play.

But we had navigated getting out of bed, meds and shower.
Now (and in less than the sometimes two hours) they were seated at the PC. Gaming, chatting, eating, smiling.
With dad, waiting in the wings, stepping into my shoes for that day.
Knowing what it was to watch others leave, whilst you stay.
Still, at the kitchen table.
Far enough away to give space,
close enough to be on hand for demands born from worry, requests, needs, and snacks.
We would hastily exit,
Lest the seeds of anxiety begin to grow.
You never know.
But for now, they were content,
So, we would go.

We drove in the sunshine

You sang,

And I smiled

Wishing all the while

That I could bottle this moment.

For darker days.

My darling love.

On our way to a Uni tour, (I pinch myself as I say it)

To explore,

and embrace new beginnings,

New paths, make plans.

A short time ago (but a whole other lifetime)

We could not see a way forward,

See the wood for the trees.

You would've clutched at my hand,

Anxiety swallowing you whole,

Brutal as quicksand...

But not that day.

And few would understand, How much that meant.

The sun was shining.

On you

My love

As you waved over your shoulder, you strode through the

gates.
Somehow taller
Somehow
Bolder.
And I turned and walked towards the river..
(Knowing that both of you were,
for now, at least,
Ok without me.)
I was alone.
Quite alone, for the first time in an age.

Like a bird free from its cage,
Not knowing where to fly
So unaccustomed to freedom
Or space to spread its wings.
A little lost, naked even,
Despite wearing 'proper' clothes
And lipstick.

My boots, new and stiff,
Never worn,
took me onwards
Towards the river,
People,
Shops,
Sunshine.
A stark contrast to the secular existence

That was, and is, our life
The sound of voices, talking,
laughing
And music
Drifted on the river breeze
And wrapped itself around me.

I breathed it in
I breathed.

The delicious aroma of hot chips lead me to a new cafe,
Where I bought some food and tried to remember how to pass the time of day,
Small talk an art I rarely used anymore
I headed for the door.

"Dancing in the moonlight" the busker sang
As the sun shone from a clear blue sky.
It took me back,
To days gone by.

I smiled
For a while
I smiled

Whilst I looked to the future
Dared to hope and to dream I felt no longer invisible,

(Or a shadow of the woman that I had once been)

An inevitable change,
When I'd helped them survive?
And I felt, and looked different
Would not hide in disguise.

And for those few moments,
With the sun warming my face,
And the music mingling with the lapping waves on the river bank,
Eating food straight from the paper
(Smothered in salt and vinegar...)

My soul was nourished
I felt like me.
Not the old me,
The me before.
But the me I had become
Battle scars and all
Wearing lipstick
Eating hot chips
Standing on the river wall.

Her hair

My beautiful daughter has a complex relationship with her hair.
It is naturally curly, and falls in ringlets of auburn, blonde and chestnut brown.
A mane of vibrant colour, texture and shape.
Mirroring her soul.

For years, at secondary school she glued it back in a tight ponytail.
Plastered to her scalp with product, crushing and flattening it to replicate the 'in' style. Masking and internalising her authenticity, her unruly locks just wouldn't do.
Uncomfortable in her own skin
As she tried so hard to fit in.

Until she could not go on.
Or brush her hair.
It hung in knots about her face, as she stayed in her chair.
In her room.
Her hair wild and free from confines, but lost.
She was unable to care for it, instead it became functional.
A screen, a mask to hide beneath.

But as winter gave way to spring, it brought with it her awakening.

And as she began the journey of freeing herself from the shackles of her pre-diagnosis identity,
She took the radical decision to cut her hair short, cast aside the mane.
And start again.

So, her hair, has grown with her, these past few years.
No longer crushed and flattened, she has learned to embrace the bounce,
The spring and the volume!
She washes, and bathes it in sweet smelling conditioners of Banana or coconut.
And it basks in its new found freedom.
Her hair glistens and shines, iridescent in the sunlight, framing her now smiling face.
And she wears it with pride as a part of who she is.
It will not be confined or tamed,
It falls haphazardly about her shoulders, curls
In defiance of a memory.
Saying
This Is me. ♥

Tonight, my daughter asked me to wash her hair.
This I gladly did.
As I ran the conditioner through her curls,
the way I used to years ago,
she looked up at me and said,

"Thank you mum. I feel my hair is quite a sacred part of me at the moment.

Thank you for helping me take care of it so well"

♥

Christmas lights

Christmas lights, warm and white, twinkling.

Paper snowflakes,

Crisp, frosty mornings

The season of cosy reds,

Greens and golds

Wreaths embellished with bows and bells

Indulgent foods

Delicious smells.

And yet

We tread a tightrope of tinsel that could break any time.

The pressure to be happy,

To be grateful

To smile

Can mean it's not so much festive cheer

But more

Of

A trial.

And so

It may snow,

Be merry,

Be pretty and white.

Or

It may all just melt

To grey mush
And that
Is
Alright.

So, we listen,
And we tweak things
Make the season our own.
Let go of expectation
(Which can be hard)
We don't have to have turkey
Or crackers
Or cards.
We acknowledge our sadness
Give voice to our grief
A bespoke yuletide season (safe and individual)
And turn over
New Leaves.

It's OK to acknowledge
Traditions we miss
But we cannot dwell
On the things
That weren't meant for our list.

We make our own new traditions
Find joy in chocolate (or sherry!)

We accept anger or sadness,
And may yet feel merry
Whilst we may not see our families
Or have friends round for mulled punch
We take heart in those nearest,
Eat our own favourite lunch
We can still find connection,
If not face to face
Beyond phone screens,
Far and wide
Out in cyber space

So, we share, and we learn
We're not the only ones after all
Who didn't have Christmas parties
Or Carol concerts at school
Together we're stronger
Whether sad,
Merry,
Or bright,
It's alright.
And we've got you,
We get it
We're here.
No pressure to perform
Or to feign Christmas cheer
Just do yuletide your own way

Knowing we will be too

From our home to yours

A peaceful Christmas to you

Anecdotes from Neurodivergent family life…

This will make you laugh. They asked for porridge and I felt like Goldilocks as the first bowl was too hot then the 2nd bowl was too cold, there don't seem to be any objections for the 3rd.

I am now waiting for the big bad wolf!

―――――

Setting an exact time to stop gaming makes my brain say no regardless of what the thing is I'm doing, pda does that mum. Instead of that, let's try agreeing a half hour slot, and I come off at some point during that time. It gives me choice and makes my body calmer.

―――――

It's never boring going shopping with C, in one shop she adjusted a mannequin's finger into a rude gesture, and in the carpark, she was thrilled to find the most beautiful stick (branch!) to take home. We only went in three shops, and she didn't choose anything, but was so happy to find things for her sibling and to take her giant stick home!
I offered her Fries and a burger, but she opted for a box of doughnuts to take home "Burger would just be for me, these we can all share "

So today has been interesting. My lovely autistic/ADHD young person has been meeting tutors for online learning.

The whole process is surreal. Educational speed dating!

So, they looked at profiles and we arranged video chats with a few to see if they clicked. There were two lessons and two chats today.

Topics covered by my wonderful young person included:
    Regional accents, " Are you Scottish?" (Does impression)
    " I will guess your age; you might not like it!"
    " Do you know anything about relevant gaming servers?"
    " Which genre of music is your favourite?"
    " You have an impressive beard"
    " You look like the dad in Shazam!"
    " Too many steps in fractions fall out of my brain"
    " The Queen is single you know but you wouldn't want to be a gold digger"
    " What would be your dream car but one that realistically is within your reach?"
    " So, are you neurodiverse?" (Explains neurodiversity)
    " I'm autistic and have ADHD, I have the whole package going on!"

There was also some fraction work, an intro to guitar and an intro to space in science.

So, people may want to bomb us. We have David Attenborough.

Enough said.

———

Me: I found your doll!

Daughter: He was buried under the kitchen sink for a reason. Look at him, he's freaky. How the F did you not guess I was different? What 'normal' child asks for a weird ass doll like that for her 12th Birthday?!

Me: So, do you want him or not?

Daughter: Yes (reluctantly) he can join Dobby with the eyes that look into your soul and the other weirdo crew in my room.

Today she has left you

Today she has left you,
Shed her tears and stepped fourth,
At a crossroads in life,
now equipped with self-worth.

This young woman before me,
Full of kindness and grace,
Shines with strength and new courage,
She has found in this place.

The walls may be shabby,
And the carpet threadbare,
But there's knowledge and passion,
In those who teach there.

Miraculous changes,
Since that first time we met,
Bravely sharing her story,
Scars she couldn't forget.

As we spoke, she fell silent,
As she shed silent tears,
The harsh realisation
of all those long-lost years.

But then she found this place,
And all that it meant
A safe space to discover
Her own will and intent

And as she felt safer,
The light in her grew
The spark burned ever brighter
And that started with you

She cast off the straight jacket
Of doubts, fears and belonging
And replaced it with colour
Vibrant outfits so stunning

She found self-expression,
Friendship and more
She found new parts of herself,
When she stepped through that door

She danced and she laughed
And sometimes still cries
But learned that is ok
With kind hearts on your side

She found inner strength
And began planning for pleasure!

Her lists, hopes and dreams
Are our greatest treasure

She came here so lost
Beaten down by a system
Failings so many
I can't even list them

But now she stands stronger
Head held high; she stands tall
Has her dreams to pursue
Thanks to you all.

Xx

The place without boxes

A welcome,
Kind words,
Introductions,
Hello's
Some sharing of stories
These people- they know...
Our children so different
In so many ways
Gender identity?
Oh, not in our day!

Seen so many closed hearts
So many closed minds
Unwilling to learn
But look and you'll find

The courage and strength
Our children possess
To break free of the confines
Not to hide with the rest

A rainbow of colour
Of hopes and of dreams
Identities, genders
And what it all means

Our children are learning
To embrace who they are
To fly their own flag
To follow their star

But this journey's not simple
It's a quest all its own
Plagued by ignorant voices
They can feel so alone.

Teenage angst over image
Is it ok to like her?
I'm supposed to like him?
It's all such a blur

'Professionals' then add their noise to the song
Tick male or female.
But I can't, am I wrong?

You see there's no box
They can put this child in.
Break the box
Smash them all
Then we can begin

A place without boxes
No need to conform
Where to be vibrant and different Is the new kind of norm

These children aren't new
They've always been there
But were hidden away
With no place they could share

This new generation
Are climbing a wall
To announce who they are
And with pride they'll stand tall

Knowing we are behind them
Every step of the way
Ready to challenge and educate
Each 'not in my day'

And when we become tired
When the journey is tough
Our tribe will remind us
That we are enough

For when we join forces
Start a new dialogue
They can shine their true light

Find a way through the fog

They can smash all the boxes

Closed hearts, bigotry

Then our children can say

"I am proud to be me."

Snapshot of a morning

1am bedtime...the need for quiet solitude outweighed the exhaustion.
A little escapism, an absorbing drama and respite.
Late night.

3am I'm woken with a plaintive cry.
The youngest is awake having flashbacks to school trauma.
Can't settle.
Scenarios play over and over in their head.
Still have a baby monitor
So, I always hear
And they know
If they need me
I will always come
Try a podcast
Try a cuddle
After an hour we give up and go downstairs so the stims don't wake the others.

4am dozing restlessly
On the sofa
Dogs stretching and sniffing
Youngest gaming to occupy their mind
And leave no space for intrusive thoughts to fill.

7am awake and up

Again

bring them cereal and meds

Boil the kettle, tea for the sleeping ones

Stoke up the coffee machine

It's already been a long day

8am youngest in the shower after returning to bed

To watch videos

Oldest one eager to be up and ready

Needs routine

Plates start spinning

9am Youngest still in shower OCD not so great today.

Wiping

Changing clothes and towels

Counting rituals..

Until they feel safe enough to venture forth and get dressed

Popping in on oldest one

Helping her find the jeans she needs In her jumbled drawers

Talking through the morning

Keeping her on track, grounding techniques calm and centred

For now

9:30am Youngest now dressed

After the pants fiasco.

(The ones they wore yesterday

And were fine

Today feel like razor blades)

meltdown

And punching

Slowly subside

As the dog licks their face

Changes the pace

And the focus

10am Downstairs the curtains are closed

The youngest one hates daylight

And fears the outside

The fireplace flickers

The fairy-lights twinkle

Needs cosy warmth

To feel safe

The oldest however craves nature and outdoors so the sun streams in

Through the kitchen window

Warming her face

As she eats her cereal.

Dog on her feet

Calming the beat

Of her heart.

Youngest is gaming

(With Second breakfast and water)

Online friends a lifesaver

In so many ways

Fill their days with chat

And laughter

Keeping the loneliness they feel so acutely at bay.

The computer, a window

To another world

One beyond these four walls

That both protect and hold them captive

Can't go outside

A lockdown imposed

By trauma and fear

They must stay

In

Here.

10:15 am Oldest is ready

Coat on and boots

Dogs are yapping their enthusiastic

Chorus of excitement..

A walk!

The one time in the day

I can feel fresh air

Wind in hair

See the birds, the trees
The carpets of leaves
As the dogs leap and play.
And as we walk
She talks
Her dreams, plans and sadness
Sometimes her gladness
Like today.

" Mum if you'd have told me a couple of years ago as I sobbed in the car, battling to try to go to school, that I could be here like this, I wouldn't have believed it. Here I am despite all of that, with my GCSEs, and I'm doing A Levels, in my way. Walking my dogs at my leisure...and listening to my body. Resting when I need to. Because now I can. Now I can hear it in a way I just couldn't before."

And I'm floored, by her wisdom. We head home
To jump through the hoops at OCD's command
Showers a must before we set foot in the same room as the youngest.
Who is gaming.
But aware its nearly
Their
Lesson.

11am Oldest changed and reset

Goes down stairs to get her water

And snack

In readiness for her lesson.

Thank goodness for zoom.

She can learn from her room.

Feeling safe

Can study in her own space

There was no other place

That would've worked.

For her.

Downstairs their lesson begins English today

With some interesting questions!

Did I mention

This one need to know, it all.

It goes something like this:

" Have you ever knocked anyone out?"

" Do you use scissors to trim that beard"

"What is your least favourite fruit?"

"Have you ever been attacked by a goose?"

I smile, and bring snacks and water.

Then try in this tiny window

To answer emails,

To make calls

And sort laundry

And cook lunch

And realise

I didn't brush my hair.

And it's only lunchtime.

Halfway

There

Doing it your way

It's been such a turbulent few years.
So many changes to navigate.
Doors closed and others opened.
Through it all, fairly silent and stoic,
You've been there,
figuring it all out, in your own way.

Sometimes you mess it up.
And storms erupt.
I'll ride the shock waves,
smoothing, calming, knowing you're sorry.
You make mistakes, because you don't yet know how to be 3
steps ahead…always.
Hypervigilance,
the adrenalin dance,
I know so well.

And, I know I get frustrated
when you don't just know their triggers the way I do.
But how could you?
I'm with them dawn till dusk.
Know their highs and lows,
even tone, gently, gently, low demand.
It's a different way of being.
It takes practice, guidance,

knowledge (so much reading and researching...in the half light, at night)
And I've come to know, that is my role, and it's why sometimes only mum will do.
But there's also you.

You don't talk or share,
so I'm not sure who's there,
when you need to vent, to shout?
So, it often comes out
Towards me.
The things you once found endearing,
Not so much anymore.
Easily angered, frustrated or sad.
Holding it in.
Until you can't.

I cry, but let it go
It'll pass,
The words hang in the air,
and I know that your anger is not really for me,
But for the illness,
And what its done...
But I'm the nearest one.
I try to help you learn,
Yearn, for you to pick up the book
I left out with hope,

Read the articles or posts that might, just might
Shed some light.

But it's just not your way.
And yet you stay.

I'm always the nearest one,
For them.
But not you.
In shouting distance,
A helicopter mum not through choice but necessity
That's me.

And you watch from the ground
As I hover.
Fuel tank on empty
Rota blades spinning,
Spinning.

You must stifle your urges
Your will to protect
And find another way
To say
I'm here I care I'm in.

And you do.

You say it with the chocolate
You just know that I'll need
Prawn cocktail crisps
Cream for my coffee...
Or with your trip to buy the specific brand of shower gel, pants
or cheese that will feel 'right.'
You might say it spending hours working,
So that I can be at home

Or by saying nothing at all,
When I order 5 dresses
in case one feels alright, and Anxiety allows her
To go to the ball.

Missed family outings
Missed time with me
You make your sacrifices
Too.

You,
are just doing it your way.

Anecdotes from Neurodivergent family life…

The Heart of the Bread (Whilst making bread)
So, what makes the bread rise? The yeast
So, the yeast is alive?

We yes but not as a living, feeling being more as a reaction.
It's moving
It's not moving

It's breathing. It's alive so it still has feelings Well no. It has no brain or nerves or heart. Yes it does.
And the yeast is the heart of the bread!
♥

Today we left the house with a spring in our step! My youngest on a high from finding out they have secured the farm placement for September, and heading there today for two blissful hours of snakes, goats, pigs and many other animal friends. On our journey, they played the music. It struck me how very different their playlist has become.
In the dark days, the 'just touch the gate' type days, they would blast angry anthems, as they donned their emotional armour and readied themselves for the hostilities ahead in their school day. The songs were a battle cry, shouted with angst and against the futility they felt in their quest for acceptance and understanding. The windows would rattle and the bass beat

through our chests as we drove into that car park.

Today they sang Lizzo. Good as hell. Smiling and laughing, performing the song with feigned painted nails and tossing non-existent locks! The music was loud, heads turning at the traffic lights loud. This was the soundtrack of triumph and the songs of tangible change. Their musical tastes are very eclectic, so we had some Oasis and Embers (our, in their opinion, very underrated '21 Eurovision entry) and a bit of Sam Ryder 'Spaceman' for good measure. All sung at max volume and with all round performance in full flow.

This is the child who only weeks ago, could not see a future, could not open the curtains, or the window.

And today, I've watched them beaming with pride as they fed the reptiles and stroked the pigs. In the sunshine.

This is the power of the RIGHT provision.

———

To make you smile. Bedtime conversation tonight consisted of (among other topics) 911

Son's English teacher's voice making her sound constipated.

A zeedonk (son announced it is a thing)

The jobs of red and white blood cells and…why some women fry and eat their placenta.

———

Today I will be going to the bathroom in the guise of a baby giraffe. I will need marks for movement and sounds.

Today's gem

Daughter (17) eating pizza at kitchen table. Has left a crust on the side.

YP (14) enters kitchen, approaches her and gives spontaneous hug (RARE OCCURRENCE) And says,

" You smell nice"

(This is a big deal, as the hair products/deodorants etc she uses trigger sensory overload in them and yesterday they kept telling her she smelled awful.

Daughter is really touched.

YP then steals prized pizza crust and legs it!

Daughter, although indignant says how lovely the hug was and how impressed she was that they stole her half-eaten pizza...as she's all too aware that their OCD would usually prevent this.

YPs chicken goujons are ready and Daughter helps herself to one (waving it proudly at them and delighting in their feigned rage)

" This is literally the best tasting chicken! It must be because it's a revenge goujon!"

😆😆😆🖤

I sometimes feel that my entire life Is Rachel making trifle

The phone

An early start

(After a late night)

For some quiet, and coffee.

Time for me.

Before…

Morning routines,

green tea with honey and a kiss for one,

For the other

Juggling, singing,

eye spy on the duvet cover

Cereal in bed

And meds.

Transitions take time

No short cuts or straight lines

Bed to bathroom

With a joke, or a song

To move things along

One in the shower

(After an hour)

The other is dressed

And trying her best

Make up

Jeans

She means business today.

We've planned a trip out
Just she and I
Some time away from the circus
Just us,
To be.
Free.

One is ready
Nerves a little unsteady
But dressed and bag packed
Has a drink and a snack
The other in towels
On the bed
Holding their head
Curled into a ball
Looking so small.

And it all comes undone

With the words:
'Don't go mum
I need you!
I'm scared!
I can't do this alone
Please just stay home'

Then despite knowing it's futile
I try for a while
To reason, reassure
To talk strategies
Techniques
But anxiety peaks
Can't talk anymore

On the floor
One on the floor
The other ready by the door.

And in that moment I miss
Our life before all of this,
Heartbreak.
Before anxiety ruled
And our world became small.

The fear becomes anger
The panic now fight
Fewer words
For a while
(Dodging the missiles)
Think on my feet
Whose needs I can meet,
First

The storm begins to subside.

Now she's not here by my side
As we planned

Instead, she sits on her bed
Reluctantly thinking
what could we do instead?

She heard all their tears has felt the same panic,
The terror so manic
Knows the dread,
But today
they feel it instead

So, despite best laid plans
The make-up,
The clothes,
She knows.

When their fear is so loud
A fear like her own
Plans have to change
You can't be alone.
Or even with dad
Because although it feels sad

Sometimes,
In the darkest moments
Only
Mum
Will do.

And a fragile calm is restored
Once they know
We
Won't go.

They are now settled and eating
A cooked breakfast to munch through
Knowing that today
they don't have to fight their demons
Without me too.

And, striking with the iron now cold I don't chastise or scold them
Instead talking of small steps
We can take next

Towards time apart
When their heart
Feels
Stronger

Then up the stairs,
My heart heavy
And full
of unshed tears
God it's been years!
How much more can we bear?

Then
She's there.
She's smiling
Arms open
She holds me and I her
No words,
I need
To follow her lead.

Despite her foiled plans
For our day out together
She knows
It won't be this way forever
And whilst her wings are clipped by
Circumstance
She's learned to dance to another tune.
She scoffs at my apology
And she shares her analogy
 And
just wow!

"You see it's like how,

There are moving staircases In a magical castle.

You step on going one way

But it moves

changes direction

Like today.

And as the staircase twists

And turns

You learn,

To embrace

the new place where you find yourself

(Other dreams on the shelf

For another

Day.)

So, you see Mum it's ok!

We can still just go for a walk

We can still talk.

That's where the staircase took us today. "

My heart bursts

Jaw on the floor

In total awe

Of the wisdom she holds

Her words still unfold.

"We'll take joy

In the small things

Today

The ones others don't see,

Lolloping dogs

Autumn leaves

Dewy cobwebs

You

and me.

It won't always be this way

Our plans can wait

For another day"

So, we hug

Then find boots

We don't need the car

Not going far

Today

And her wise words

Resound

Her thoughts so profound "This is not our forever,

But, we ride the moving staircase,

Because..

We're all in this together"

♥♥♥

Self care

Morning coffee

Quiet

Chill, crisp air

Dew

Birds singing

Clouds dancing

Hot tea

Biscuits

Bacon

Stroking the dog

Favourite song on the radio

Brushed hair

Clean skin

Fresh breath

Clean clothes

Cosy socks

A smile

A hug

A glance

A glimpse of them.

Calm after storm

Ice cold water

Stretchy pants

Comfort food

Stroking the dog

Texting a friend

Writing

Reading (if you can)

Stroking the dog

Stroke the dog

The dog.

The cola bottle

Many of you may be familiar with the cola bottle effect. An analogy used to explain to others the build-up and impact of challenges (shake the bottle) throughout the school day for a ND child, which finally causes the cola to explode, representing the meltdown.
It struck me today; I've never read an adult version...
Here's mine.

You start the day already tired.
Although you were exhausted, you had desperately needed alone time to reset. The children didn't settle until after 11.30pm last night, which meant that you finally gave in and fell into bed around 1am, youngest was restless all night, so your sleep was broken by your hyper-vigilance.
Woken at 6am by the dog needing the loo.

Shake the bottle.

Your morning ritual of coffee, in your special, chipped, but much loved, Christmas mug is de-railed. Out of coffee.
Meant to buy it yesterday.

Shake the bottle.

Realise there are several other grocery items you need to buy today, whilst navigating if, and when, you can leave your ND teens, depending on how they're doing.
And damn it, the bread is mouldy. Seriously, you wonder wtf is wrong with you and why you can't run a house like other mums.

Shake the bottle.

You wake the kids, bringing meds and breakfasts (different for each in their specific bowls with their specific spoons) singing songs to raise spirits and listening to them sharing their dreams.
The dog vomits.
You clean it up whilst realising you need to chase up the pet insurance company about the vet bill, but it's fourth on your list of important phone calls and the others must be done today. The thought of calling the SEN department to hound them, again, over meeting your child's needs literally churns your stomach.

Shake the bottle.

You co-regulate and navigate the youngest's morning shower. OCD demanding you get dressed at speed, between wiping the bathroom floor and fetching clean towels. Timing is everything. If you're out, so will they be. It matters to you that you support them, they are trying so hard. Where the hell is the red towel?

Shake the bottle

Shower completed for one, your eldest needs sensory support over a mysterious scent that's triggering her.
You can't locate it and try to help her reset by opening windows and putting on the fan. But you know she's still struggling and you can't help fix it. In frustration she pushes you away, verbally. You understand why, but your heart just hurts as you step away to give her space.

Shake the bottle

You answer emails about psychology appointments and physio appointments, whilst preparing the 3rd micro breakfast of the day (no mushrooms, squashy Avocado, and the right kind of ham. Not for you. You don't feel hungry, and yet you can't fit your bloody jeans anymore! You don't feel you know this body, this stomach.

Shake the bottle.

Your spouse comments, very innocently, that the oven is smelly and needs cleaning.
You're acutely aware of the acrid smell.
However, your children don't go to school. They are always

here, at home.
Neither can cope with the sensory overload of the chemical small of oven cleaner. So you've wiped and cleaned as best you can, but it still smells. You feel it as a judgement.

Shake the bottle.

You need to get changed (their OCD triggered again- you walked the dog, you're contaminated) but after the 5th change of outfit, you stand in your mismatched underwear no closer to finding something that doesn't make you feel ten years older than you are. Or that clings to your stomach, loudly announcing your weight gain.You can't find an outfit that feels like you. Because you don't know what 'you' feels like anymore.

Shake the bottle.

By the afternoon you're bubbling.
Trying to keep putting one-foot in front of the other.
The moments of triumph and joy with your wild ones, stave off the impending explosion for a while.
It helps when you smile.
Then the bins need emptying, the laundry needs folding, the new load needs hanging and the dog needs it's food.
The dishwasher needs reloading, the 10th snack needs preparing, the daughter needs reminding to keep hydrating (without sounding like a demand) Darling would you like some

ice in your drink..?

Damn it, the shopping. You're out of the pasta they'll eat!

Shake the bottle.

You walk into the doorframe.

Shake the bottle.

You trip over the stairs, and drop the laundry you were carrying.

Shake the bottle.

Youngest needs the bathroom.
It'll be at least an hour.
You're required to be outside the door.
But you must not speak.
Or move.

Shake the bottle.

An hour in, the eldest now needs the loo.
But if you speak to the youngest, or try to hurry them, they'll become more stuck.
So, you wait it out, stifling the building scream, because the eldest needs your composure and support.

Shake the bottle.

Dinner is ready, the alarm you set just went off but you're still stuck outside the bathroom.

Shake the bottle.

Much later, after co regulating youngest through an OCD shower meltdown, rather bruised, you make it back to the kitchen.
Where you realise that lunch needs prepping for youngest's Farm visit tomorrow. The one time in the week they leave the house. And they need their white, crusty roll for lunch.
But you were unable to go to the store today, as the need was too high. So, your spouse kindly went. But bought floppy rolls (crusty all gone, you know it's your fault as you should have thought about this yesterday, damn your memory.) They were trying to help, and you're thankful, you are. But, these rolls are not ones your youngest will eat. So, you know you'll be doing a late night grocery dash, like some kind of stealth like ninja parent, getting out and back before you're missed.

Shake the bottle.

Your head hurts and you wonder why? Then remember you haven't had a drink for hours.
And oh yeah, you still need to pee. So, you go to the bathroom

and clean the sodden floor. Replace the toothpaste and wipe the mirror.
Then go down stairs and realise you still need to pee, what the hell is wrong with you?

Shake the bottle.

Then the toast burns.

And the bottle explodes.

Internally.

Silent sobs that hurt your throat as you swallow them into your clenched stomach (and you wonder why you're never hungry?!) And rock, gently on the kitchen floor.

The tears won't stop.

Stupid toast.

The dog licks your face, wagging his tail and sitting on your feet. You bury your face in his fur and breathe in his reassuring scent. feel the weight of him against you.

And breathe.

Breathe.

Breathe.

Your daughter sends you a funny meme with a kiss.

You see in the kitchen, your husband bought you a crazy, random gnome for your garden.

You smile.

Reset.

Breathe.

'Mum, mum!'

Shake the bottle....

The green flags

The key sits in the lock of the open window
Not hidden on a shelf.
The curtain billows in the breeze,
Dancing in celebration.
Liberation.
The handwash is still two thirds full!
Has it been a week?
And there's a spare in the cupboard, untouched!
A bottle a day seems so long ago,
And yet like yesterday.

When it was all just too much

Too much.

The towels are dry!
Resting at length between uses,
(Rather than constantly damp,
Sodden with angst, soaked from their cries)
No fourth shower, just morning and night.
And if we're lucky, they'll sing.
On a good day, they just might.

These are the green flags.

The life buoys.

At last.

Recovery is not linear, were told all the time.
Set-backs are part of the voyage.
Be patient.
Find joy.

Look for the life buoys!
The current is strong,
To fight it is futile.

So instead, we swim with the tides...
Whether tranquil
Or tempest.
And we celebrate change,
(Imperceptible to outsiders.)
And rest.
With the knowledge
That we're moving.

A smile.
A song
An open window.
A dog walk.

Less soap.

Green flags,

Hope.

Peppered with challenge,
Obstacles and storms,
This voyage is theirs to navigate,
We,
Must
Wait.
(Patiently)

They'll weigh up their options
In time, set their own course.
Tread water or swim?
It's for them to decide

Through unexplored waters
Tranquil or rough,
It is enough

That they know,
That you'll swim by their side

(Watching out for green flags!)

Cold coffee and Carparks

In the car park the sun is shining through the windscreen,
warming the seats,
melting the chocolate on my biscuits.
My treat,
my celebration that we've come so far on this journey.

Outside
Pigeons
bobbing,
fluttering ,
comically scavenging for crumbs.
The ivy swaying gently as the fence creaks in time.

Cars come and go.
People chatter, small children skip from the confines of their
car seats and bounce a ball as they head to the park.
Simply, naturally... with ease they go and play.
Free from the claws of anxiety, they have evaded them thus
far..they skip merrily away.

But I stay.
In my car.
In the carpark.
She knows I am here, and that is enough.

I stay.
I am the safe space.
The getaway driver.
The security guard.
The anchor yet by my actions, the liberator.

So I stay...

Families bicker, dogs frolic in anticipation of their run in the park, leaping from their cars they yap excitedly, tugging their owners forward.
Bounding with mischief and promise...they go.

But I stay.
I stay in the car.

I sit in the car park.
Stationary.
Sitting.
Waiting.
And in doing so, she finds her courage and moves on.
She moves forward.
The irony apparent to us both, but we pay it no heed.
For we know what she needs.
And nothing else matters, so as others chatter and go...I stay.

I do it gladly, staying here, in this car, with the sun shining through the windows..a gift and an honour to be asked to join her.
For so long she stood still.
Still.
Enveloped by sadness.. and now its my turn to stand still, to help free her.

I am inert, stationary...watching, heart in throat as she takes those first tentative steps away, steps forward towards freedom, she takes those steps, not without fear, heart pounding in her ears, but she goes, as she knows...
That I will stay
in the carpark.

How many car parks have I seen? I wonder as scroll back through the dark months. Memories resonate through me , turning my stomach, regret claws at my heart.

The school car park.
That was where it began.
The waiting.
In tears.
Head in hands.
Stomach in knots.
Having handed her over.

In tears at the office to the teacher with the saccharine sweet voice.
Being told is was the 'right thing to do' before I knew better.
Before I questioned, listened, learned.
Stood shoulder to shoulder with my beautiful, brave girl and said no more.

The school car park at the end of the day, being there 30 minutes early to ensure I could park in the right space for her.
She survived a whole day.

Waiting in anticipation I ask myself if thats a good thing?
She stumbles out, weary, her mask slipping slightly.
I wrap her in my arms, my love, trying in vain to undo the damage done that day. Knowing that she's done for the week, she has nothing left and will be an unauthorised absence tomorrow.
Again.

The school car park when we call it .
We stop it.
No more.
We are done.
The day she collapsed in the 'wellbeing' room clinging to the radiator, being told to stop it, to calm down as she gasped for air in that place of hostility and entrapment.

As the SENDCo questioned the validity of her tears with no diagnosis or proof.
No more.
It stopped there but not soon enough.
No, not soon enough.
They took her apart piece by piece, the system, the policies, the rules.
 The prison they called 'school'.

The car then remained still for some time.

 Standing sentry on our drive as we fought to find her.
To help her find herself.
We were stationary for some time.

The chocolate has melted.
Discarded, as I scan the car park.
Always watching, my engine running, ready to catch her if she falls.
But to my relief there's no sign.

People come and go, friends chatting, greeting hugging, heading off for lunch.
I stay.

Car parks, places to stop and wait.

Yet some are simply the beginning of a journey. we parked in the wrong one that day, the day she started on her new road. Her own road.

A smiling Dr, reassuringly scatty and eccentric, she saw her with the clarity others had lacked.

She gave her the tools to learn to fix the broken parts.

Roadside recovery for the soul.

Uncharted territory, the road less travelled.

We set off together.

So now I sit and wait on this journey and soak up every minute of the glorious view. Stationary but moving forwards all the time .

Gaining momentum... now that she is in the driving seat, changing gear or direction as and when she needs.

Breaking when she tires and learning to listen to the warning signs when she needs to refuel.

On this ever undulating journey.

Dogs bark loudly, announcing their presence.

Paws caked in mud, tails wagging furiously they pile into their car and head home.

And I wait, relief and excitement mounting with each passing minute on the clock.

I scan the car park.

No sign.

These days so mundane and 'normal' to so many.

Whilst in my mind this little trip means so much.

My beautiful daughter has gone to meet a friend.

For coffee, and a chat.

SHE HAS GONE TO MEET A FRIEND !

I want to shout my joy and pride and adoration to the world.

But the pigeons are not interested as they waddle, feasting on the discarded cookie of a carefree child.

In the carpark.

And all at once she's there.

I barely recognise the confident young woman striding towards the car.

Head high, defiant , challenging the demons that held her captive for so long.

A smile dances around her eyes, lighting up her face, making this carpark , in this moment, the most beautiful place in all the world to me.

I wait, as she climbs in, talking excitedly about her morning... the wheels begin turning but the world stands still... as I drink in every minute of this triumph.

No words needed for she knows without a doubt ,that while she finds her feet, explores the world once more...

I will gladly wait in carparks watching, as she opens up her door.

♥

Mother

Many talk of gratitude.
Many talk of closeness,
Of companionship,
Friendship even, when they speak of their mothers.

I knew little of that, it was not a picture that was true, for me.
The utter adoration I'd felt when young,
Had given way to distance,
Tumultuous teens and circumstance,
Grown apart.

But there was still heart.

It is said, that there are silver linings.
That from the darkness, shards of light can be found, for those who look.

It took this sadness,
This dark and lonely chapter,
For me to see her
Again.

There was a day, I felt so small.
Overwhelmed by the weight of this fight,
The futility, washed over me

As I struggled to swim against the tide.
No one by my side
That day.

I had reached out, I'd called.
And as I sat, enveloped in sadness.
I found comfort,
In the voice of my mother.
Another day, a new start.
No grand gestures for us
But it was enough, to hold space.
A place,
To begin.

With renewed authenticity,
Came sharing,
And honesty.
Grandmother to my daughter,
I watched them,
Find their way.

Their closeness, it touched me,
It gladdened my heart,
Made me smile.
And after a while,
It struck me.

On this messy journey

Travelling companions are few,

There is no plan, map or guidebook.

Those around us, are our compass

As we travel towards a brighter horizon.

And look,

Forward, ahead

Not behind or instead

Sinking under the weight

Of the darkness.

As our train leaves the station,

We know not destination,

Or indeed who will be with us, still, as we find our feet

But we do know of love,

Of shared vision,

Direction.

As our train leaves the station

Mother now takes her seat.

X

Someone else's day

Today was the dreaded day.
The optician appointment.
She hadn't slept for three nights, in constant fear of this day.
Her anxiety so heightened that her body had gone into survival mode, with blood rushing to sustain her organs whilst her hands and feet turned blue.
This was not new.
We have learned the many ways her body responds when under perceived threat.
If we could just get there, it might be OK.
Wrapped in layers, shaking, heating and music providing some comfort on the journey.
Car parked.
Mask on.

Hand in hand walking to the optician.

Aware that at any moment we may have to turn back, without judgement and try another day.
But, today, she made it!
Pre-test assessment, done.
In the chair, ashen face, can't stand this place.
Bright lights in her eyes are her nemesis, so the challenge was immense.
Test complete, the colour returned slowly to her face.

Smiling optician advised on frames and she chose a pair (quickly, I knew she was nearing her limit and was anxious to leave) and we were handed over to a stern-faced assistant. Brusque in tone and devoid of smile.
It took a while.
The computer was down.
And then came the lesson.
You see I felt irritation, frustration, judgement even of the assistant and her stern demeanour.

She, on the other hand said
" I love your nails, they're such a beautiful colour"
And with those words, the sun came out!
The assistant thanked her, and smiled, then shared that she had them specially painted for her Birthday just passed.

She responded with " Happy Belated Birthday"
The sun shone even brighter, and the assistant went on to share that her nails matched the stone in her engagement ring. Further pleasantries were exchanged, and she, now pink cheeked and smiling signed the forms herself and arranged her glasses collection, with the support of the now beaming assistant.. who thanked her for her custom and shared that she was now going to lunch!

"Thank-you, and enjoy your food, you deserve it!" were her parting words.

She left the opticians inches taller, warm and smiling.

"That lady was clearly having a tough day, she just needed someone to be kind. I think I cheered her up."

I genuinely had a lump in my throat.
Despite the challenges she had faced, she had still looked for opportunities to spread happiness.
To bring joy.

She collapsed into the car, and once home she shut down.
Reminiscent of an appliance in need of charging.
We know now what she needs at these times, so I took her warm, green tea with honey, an extra cosy pair of socks and tucked her up with the TV remote in hand. Without speaking, she knows I understand.
Just a kiss on the forehead and a smile.
She rested a long while.
Hours to recover, as the after effects of the adrenalin slowly receded.

And I, humbled by her stoicism and kind heart, had a cup of tea. And fell apart, briefly, before drying the tears of relief and pride. Can't comprehend the strength she holds inside.

Today was the dreaded day.
The optician appointment.

She hadn't slept for three nights in constant fear of this day.

She had started shaking, cold and quaking

And emerged accomplished

(Now exhausted)

Glowing cheeks,

from making

Someone else's day.

The kindness of strangers

There will always be much talk
Of futility and fighting.
Advocacy is fraught with battles,
And disappointments,
Which in turn will change you...
As you wrestle with lies,
With policies
Figuring out
What's
True.

You, will find the once optimistic are beaten into submission,
By broken systems and services,
And those who work within them.
Exhausted by this mission.

Over time the 'Pollyannas' become more desolate.
Losing hope,
A slippery slope.

They come to anticipate,
Expect disbelief,
Dismissed and down trodden
The armour stays on,
Because the fight is the one thing that can be relied upon,

To be there.
But,
Every so often,
Comes someone who cares.

I sometimes reflect on those who passed through,
Bringing, even momentarily
Some light, some kindness, to my child.
(Even whilst wide eyed, and wild)
They knew.

Yes, they knew.

Our children,
Acutely attuned to detect the sincere,
Those with genuine hearts,
And it is with those real allies,
Reaching out,
Giving hope,
That the re-building starts.

So here,
Here is where I thank you
The kind ones who shone through
Our journey is far from finished,
But the hope that was diminished,
Grows stronger,

Thanks to you...

The fudge shop owner,
Dynamic, slightly mad.
We met him as the fog descended,
The smile hadn't fallen,
The laughter hadn't ended,
Yet.
He showed interest,
Took time to talk,
To share,
To listen,
Loved that they wanted to try,
And were keen.
You made them feel they were worth your time,
You helped
Them
Feel
Seen.

The tutor at the dance school,
Who saw the light,
The spark,
Needed more care and love than others,
To keep burning through her dark.
You took time to walk her in,

To offer her a hand.
She knew that you
Saw her,
You would understand
That she was fighting shadows,
Her report read:
I see YOU,
Come through!

The travel content couple,
A window outside our walls,
Sharing scenes of adventure,
Woodlands,
Waterfalls.
Your gentle, soft narration,
Became part of our goodnight,
And their dreams, became their hopes, their plan.
Daring to believe they might...
One day venture out,
Walk among those hills.
The message that you sent them,
Makes them smile still.

The landscape gardener
Made them part of your team,
Gave a T Shirt and acceptance
Talked of futures,

Talked of dreams.

Had them mix cement and whilst laying down the drive,

In the sunshine, exchanging banter,

They seemed at last

Alive.

The tutors who saw through you,

Learned how to reach the true you,

Nurtured trust, taught through fun

Your journey, far from over

Had at last begun...

The founder of a community

Celebrating neurodiversity,

A Beacon of hope,

In the longest of nights

Loneliness, isolation

But now they just might

Make

Some

Friends.

Find a place, to share,

Laugh,

Belong

All the while laughing

At your great lockdown song!

Not forgetting the dance coach
Who helped her to take a chance,
And break free from her chains,
So, she could once again
Dance.
And find joy,
Validation,
In a body that she knew,
Had lost something she loved
But found it again
With
You.

So, although it's cliché It really is true
To say
Look for the helpers.
Those who'll bring light
A genuine smile,
Might,
Just make the difference,

It's a start, the kind heart
...it's a reason to hope

When all else feels sad

A gesture,

A message,

You aren't all alone,

Life isn't all bad.

Have you made the phone call?

Have you made that phone-call? Are there any clean socks? Didn't know we needed milk, why didn't you ask me to get some?

Is that bin bag still by the gate? I'll put it in the bin shall I?

I'll get that oven cleaned; it's starting to smell isn't it?
Oh, is the chocolate all gone?

Oh, the sink sieve is not in properly.
Did you know it stops the sink pipe clogging up?
Did you chase up that refund email?
Do you know where that form is?

So, you don't want this soup then?
Did you mean to leave it on the hob?

The washing machine sounds strange, is it overloaded it again?
The hoover must be picking up well, it's very full isn't it?
Not wearing the dress I bought, then?

Did you hear them up at 5am?

Do you know how to calm them from trauma flashbacks that happen as you're trying to make a call?

Or navigate the bathroom with OCD nipping at your heels trying to take hold of them?

Did you know they both need support before, during and after online lessons?
(whilst you're making lunch and hanging up damp laundry)?

And water, with regular reminders to drink? And regular snacks and small meals?

And the dogs needed more chicken and rice cooked?

And they both needed CAMHS team appointments made?
Meds reviews?
EHCP meeting to gather evidence for?

Talking through her afternoon low to help her find a way forward?

That I empty the bin but can't go out of the gate or an OCD meltdown will de rail the day?

That the load of laundry has all 3 sets of clothes they'll be needing later today?

The milk was used in porridge as they could stomach dinner, but I was managing an anxiety escalation so didn't text you a shopping list?

The oven smells, but the oven cleaner is smellier and overwhelms them into sensory meltdown?

That the chocolate is all gone
Because when I was so tired I could have cried, I ate it and kept going?
And ran you a bath.
And made you a hot meal.

And I'm not wearing that dress, because I feel like an imposter in it?
That I don't need you to remind me of all the things I didn't do,
But to see the many I did.

And for you to know that whilst you can't see the woman you married,
she's here somewhere,
just trying to get them through every day.

And she loves you.
Even if she's in leggings, not a dress.

My future self

A momentary pause
And time to reflect
On a Monday
Of many colours

It started with a three hour sit in,
Frustration and angst
Eventually subsiding as they began the day.
And ate pancakes with bacon,
And tea.

And me?
 A long, awaited walk and time to talk
With my daughter.
To laugh and run
Down the street
With the dogs.

Back for a shower
Washing my hair with apple shampoo
Simple pleasures
Get you through.
Then lessons begin

English today,

New tutor, new start.
Last week was not pleasant
And left them shaking,
Re living school trauma
Not again
Not again.

And I smile as I listen.
To them singing.
Singing
And laughing.

Singing Rick Astley's
Most notable tune
Chatting and planning
And soon, the writing starts.

A Letter to My Future Self...
Dear my future self in 2030 (you probably have a flying car),
Why hello there young one, or shall I say old one. I hope you are still alive and have come over OCD and punched it in the crotch! I am currently sitting at my setup, in an English lesson while writing this to you. I hope you have not committed any crimes and withheld from being a prick. You SHALL not be in debt with the government. I also hope you are planning on moving to Brighton, as you can relax and live alone but maybe you have a partner now and start a new lease of life with family

and happiness.

And I smile, all the while thankful, that they can see a future self.

(Hopefully without crime, or being a prick!)

🖤

Anecdotes from Neurodivergent family life...

Me: your tutor is in Italy this week so will be teaching you from there.
YP: why?
Me: a holiday I think.
YP: thinking.
YP: OK. Well, you can tell him that if he's in Italy I will only be taking part in lessons if he teaches them in an Italian accent.
I think that's fair.

Upon looking through Exeter Uni website:
"Oh, my goodness mum.
Look at this professor! He literally looks like Gandhi had a baby with Dumbledore.
He's Gandhidor! Kinda sounds like a dinosaur. That alone could make you want to go there!"

Upon opening a cheese burger in a fast-food restaurant, the contents spill out: "Well, I must admit to feeling rather hoodwinked.
This doesn't vaguely resemble the picture.
They could make it more aesthetically pleasing! "
☺

Daughter (upon seeing an image of a clifftop house): That's where I am, teetering most if the time. But I like that house, can I have it?

Me: Not that easy I'm afraid. It looks pretty empty and run down too.

Daughter: I can move in and claim squatter's rights.

Me: OK

Daughter (thoughtfully): Do you actually have to squat? And for how long?

Is it like when the landlord arrives you have to assume the position to be taken seriously? (Demonstrates!)

―――――

We saw bumblebees today.

They were engaging in highly questionable activities.

―――――

What have you got there?

A bee, it died I'm afraid so I'm picking it up in case the dogs eat it.

How?

In a tissue

How did it die?

I don't know love, it's dead so I can't ask it.

What does its soul say?

House of Cards

Welcome to my house of cards,
Hyper-vigilance comes as standard
But the full panic attack
Will set you back
Somewhat.

It's not your average house,
Delicately, intricately constructed,
Bated breath,
With each card added
Adrenalin fuelled frenzy to hold it all together when one card doesn't sit
Quite
Right…

Lest it should all fall around you,

In a cataclysmic meltdown,

Coffee is on tap, and you'll convince yourself that it's helping,
fuelling your resolve,
To hold together this fragile structure
Really though, you know,
It just makes your heart race,
As you try to keep everything in place

The cards are not of Jokers, Kings and Queens
But husbands,
Dogs,
And quirky teens.
Neurodivergent needs
That overlap or clash
And the breeze of uncertainty that murmurs constant threat

Yet,

For the most part
My house of cards stands tall.

And on the days where all is well,
The 'good' days, of smiles,
Successes, and harmony
The sun streams through the cracks
Lighting up the house of cards in all its
Iridescent fragility,
Luminescent beauty.

And you allow yourself to become lost In a moment of gratitude,
Reflecting upon how far these cards have come.
No longer crumpled and bent out of shape by the rough handling of others
But tall,

Wearing the lines as battle scars,
As an ode to their strength,

You take your eye off the ball

Or rather, a wall.

It only takes one.
A moment of self-indulgent reminiscing
To bring a shift in balance.
A need not met,
An overload,
Intrusive thoughts,
It all smells wrong!

And in the blink of an eye,
And as though it happens to some dramatic song,

The House of cards collapses.

Again.

Like putting out fires, you'll find the source
Among the debris of angst and tears,
Or the dis-regulated yelling
As the others shield their ears.

The cards have fallen.

You ignore the voice,
The whispers of self-judgment,
That would chastise and reprimand.
Not today.
You're needed.

So, you drown them in more coffee,
As you roll up your sleeves
And pick up the cards
One
By
One.

You lovingly smooth them,
Uncrumple their edges
And stand them up,
With all the help they need,
Taking heed

They could fall again at any time.

Which is why,
Although risky
And self-indulgent,

Basking in the moments of perfect balance is vital.
However fragile
However transient or fleeting,

Those are the moments that fuel you,
That warm you,

As once again you re-build your
House of Cards.

Fishbowl families

Loneliness, isolation,

Exclusion

words used frequently when discussing the emotional impact

on young people of being too unwell to attend a school ,

too unwell to leave the safety of their homes,

their rooms,

or even

their beds.

Life carries on regardless.

Brutal in its depiction of normalcy.

As if watching from a fishbowl

The routines,

The mundane errands of shopping,

Meeting friends for a catch up,

Family parties

Smiles and laughter.

All there,

just beyond the glass

As you swim in circles.

You can hear it,

Smell it,

Taste it.

The freedom.

Compounding your sadness at how very small your world has become.
And your sense of invisibility to those beyond the glass...

Sadness, yes.
But resentment, no.
This is how things need to be for your young person to feel safe.
To find comfort and to begin to heal.
Your world needs to be this small for now.
Great peace is found in the predictability and sameness of your fishbowl life.

And when your stomach lurches,
your breath catches in your throat
Or your eyes leak ever so slightly,
as you watch another family event,
or friend's birthday treat pass you by,
You remind yourself that it won't always be this way.
One day, there'll be movement, there'll be change,
however slowly and however small.

And sure enough there is.

But here's the thing.
The changes you one day begin to see,
that you celebrate and welcome,
are often imperceptible to those outside the fishbowl.
So subtle, so treasured,
So invisible to those who never truly saw you and know not where to look.

And as you begin to gain some momentum and access the outside world one day at a time,
You are reminded by those you hold dearest that you no longer have a seat at their table.

Because whilst there is change, it does not mean your life or way of accessing the activities many take for granted are simple.
Your needs, or the needs of your young people, require support.
Dynamic thinking.
Acceptance and Creativity.

What would that kind of inclusion look like?

Meeting at the cafe too much? Too loud? Too busy? Too many smells?

No problem, meet in the woods for a walk. Will be so lovely to see you.

Can't make a commitment? Can't formally accept an invitation because your neuro-spicey world does not allow for pre-planning attendance at potentially anxiety inducing events? No worries, we'll put your name down and if you can make it, you'll be so very welcome.

Wouldn't it be wonderful for you and your family to be embraced.
To be held.
 To be seen.
To be included, in the wider world.

Maybe one day.

But until then, you take heart in the few but fabulous ones.
The ones who know the view from inside the fishbowl world.
Who find flexible ways to spend time with you.
Maybe through messages, or videocall.
A life line of compassion, validation and humour from one fishbowl to another.

Bringing love

Bringing shared elation as your young ones grow in confidence,
and step forwards,
Safe in the knowledge that you'll meet them where they are.

No judgement
No expectations
Just joy that today you can enjoy time together, they've taken their seat at the table.

And on the days that's too much?

Their seat can wait until they're ready.

Because in our fishbowl,
and within our community of fishbowl families,
While we wait for the world to catch up,

There are chairs for all...

(or bean bags, or gym balls or cushions....)

Muffins and sunlight

So tired.

Tired of hoping and dreaming of a brighter day only to be defeated by breakfast time.

Of knowing it's hours until bedtime so finding a way to see pockets of light and keep going.

One-foot in front of the other.

Making plans, realistic ones that could actually happen.

They're my children.

I'm their mother.

Reflecting on how far we've come instead of dwelling in the dark moments.

It's what I do. Because I love you.

So much.

But I can still love you and be tired.

Tired of carrying the load
The OCD
The relentless intrusive thoughts that plague my child and are compulsively shared with me to lessen the hold, the intensity.

I carry that load, to make theirs slightly lighter and more bearable, whilst trying to gently, compassionately and without demand or direction, teach them the tools to manage and quell that voice.
And to remind myself in the moments when their fear becomes fury, a grenade which I catch and explodes in my hands...

This is the illness. It is not their choice.

The health anxiety, gnawing at my child, causing them pain and panic, making them ill.

Still, I'm here to re assure, be the voice of reason.

Chase the demon away, or at least keep it at bay.

And so, begins another day,

I'll allow myself a cry,
Before I stand up,
Take the speckled bananas from the fruit bowl,

And begin baking muffins.

And as I do my child appears, and together we mix, as we chat, and they joke, and they smile.

I'll hold on to that moment, as it's these moments, these shafts of sun-light cutting through the dark stormy skies that restore me,
For a while.

Humour,
Connection,
being silly sustains.

Tired, so tired,
But not quite fragmented,
Cemented,
And held together,
By the smile,
However, fleeting,
Of my child.

And I remind myself, that in this house,
Although I'm so very tired, and more than a little broken in parts,
I will make muffins,
I will look for the light

And tell the ones that I love,

Each day brings a new start.

The chair

The chair stands vacant.

Now.

So much a part of her story,
An earlier chapter,
One of heartbreak
And pain.

The chair,
The bed.

Her world.

Restless nights spent in bed
With me close by,
For safety,
And comfort.
Holding her as she cried.

And by day
The chair.
Was always there as a place of sanctuary.
Her fortress,
Her boundary.

Separating day from night
She might, hold on
To some kind of pattern,
Routine.

It seemed, that way forever.

Never,
Could we have foreseen a day
Where the chair
Held her laundry Instead of her sorrow.

A tomorrow we prayed would come.
Back when the chair was both her savour
And her gaoler.
Before she found her spark,
Hidden
Under the chair
In the dark.

She would eat there,
Read there,
Try to watch a movie,
Anything to escape her thoughts.
Flickering across the screen,
Musketeers brandishing swords,
Fighting those who would betray them,

As she too fought,
Vulnerable,
Her armour in tatters,
Valiantly,
She fought on.

Until,
After many months of darkness,
Shielded from the world
By her mustard upholstered fortress,
She found a way,
Her way,
To venture forth.

Some days now I find the chair strewn with discarded clothes,
And I pinch myself to check
I'm not dreaming.

A sweater carelessly flung over the arm,
The pile of clean laundry,
Haphazardly toppling sideways
Waiting to be put away,
Brings me such joy!

There was a time you see,
When her world was small,

And the chair was
All
There
Was.

But now,
Now, the chair is part of the furniture.
Still there for her,
When she needs safety, rest
To comfort and restore

No longer a gaoler
It's the chair she walks past
With her jacket,
And bag
Heading out of the door...

Today they ate a cookie

Today they ate a cookie
As they laughed with friends and played
We really had to pinch ourselves
It hadn't always been this way

This wasn't the beginning
Nor is this the end
But rather it's a journey
That began with finding friends

The child sat alone again
Gaming on a screen
Games console for protection
Could not bear to be seen

Surrounded by four walls for safety
Trying to forget
All those that had let them down
Hurt or damaged them
And yet…

The longing for acceptance
Had still not gone away
Connection and true friendship
Eluded them until that day

A simple search online
Had flicked the switch from dark to bright
A space for them, that seemed it may
In darkness bring some light

That first chat a catalyst
A tiny spark was lit
To those who frown on screentime
They are here because of it!

No, it is not hyperbole
That connection was the start
A place to learn to trust again
And heal a saddened heart

A safe welcoming community
Of others who'd endured the jibes
From those who were ignorant
But here they'd found their tribe

Shared interests and acceptance
No need to mask or hide
Authenticity emerging
Embracing what they'd kept inside

Through the isolation and the pain
This place gave light relief
A sense of solidarity
To find their self-belief

Over months of chatting, gaming, laughing
A change in them we saw
"I'M AUTISTIC" they would proudly shout
And they wanted to know more!

There was no magic formula
The hard days still brought tears
But they were comforted by others now
Something they'd not had for years

Spectrum Gaming was the place
They first found they belonged
Friendship helped to fight anxieties
Found new ways to be strong

And when the plan to meet emerged
They'd felt joy but also fear
Anxiety and OCD
Had kept them prisoner in here

But, knowing others found it difficult
To break through their walls and fears

Had driven them to venture fourth
How they'd not done for years

So, the tribe they came, from far and wide
Stood together face to face
Many fighting demons
as they travelled to that special place

And in the woods, they laughed and climbed
As though they did this every day
And many parents looking on
Wished that it could be that way

They built fires, swung in hammocks
Making memories so strong
That would fortify and…and give them courage
Something good to build upon

When Andy bought the cookies
And they all got stuck in
This mother felt her heart contract
Is this where it all begins?

You see an act so simple
Eating food bought by another
But this was, a giant leap of faith
Hailed new horizons to discover

This meet up wasn't the beginning

Nor was it the end

But a landmark on their journey

That they now travel with friends.

Xx Thank you Andy

The window

When school stopped
So too did the breeze,
The fresh air
The light.

Windows closed
Curtains drawn
Shutting out the world
Lest it should seep inside.

It stayed that way for months
Solace in a screen
A different kind of 'windows'
Your means of connection now.

I joined you in the darkness
Bringing light in where I could.
Fairy lights, fire on,
A cosy haven from the dangers beyond the window.

And then one day,

A change.
One curtain stayed open
You let in a little sunshine.

A little sunshine

A small action
That ignited hope
It was a start
A glimmer of light

But the road to recovery
Is not a straight line
Steps forward, then back
Curtains open,
Then closed.

But gradually
Chinks of light
Become shards.
And the Curtains stay open

But the windows
Must always be closed.
No fresh air
No breeze.

A tangible safety barrier
Viewing life
From behind a pane of glass
Until, at last...

It happened

Quite unexpectedly

I didn't see it coming

And was humbled

By your bravery

I had been at the shops

When the landscaper arrived

He was working on the driveway

Behind the window

And watching

You,were inside.

He was someone you trusted

Had been one of few

Who saw you,

And helped you feel that you belonged

Were seen,

Accepted.

You had worked side by side

Before the darkness grew strong

Mixing cement

Laying foundations

In so many ways.

Seeing him there
Beyond the glass
You were reminded
Of those days

Laying bricks In the sun.

And very briefly something changed.

When I arrived home
You announced
Very calmly
(Without fanfare or fireworks)
"I opened the window mum
And made him a coffee.
We had a nice chat."

And just like that
You went back to your online world.
Having opened the window into ours.
And although closed again, for now
We had seen you knew how.

And my heart danced in the breeze
And knew the feeling of fresh air
And hope.

After the storm

Today I sit in my kitchen.
The sun streams through the open window,
Sparrows squabble on the lawn over the spilled seed,
Whilst the washing flutters on the line.

My daughter sits upstairs,
Working diligently on her English lesson,
The soothing tones of her classical study music
Harmoniously accompanying the Sparrows.

My youngest is at their desk in their outside room,
Engaged in autonomous learning about chickens...in readiness for,
And in anticipation of,
The next therapy farm trip.

It is momentarily quiet.

I can hear my heart beating.
Racing,
Pounding,
As my eyes scan the notes from yesterday's meeting.

Words dance around the page,
Five words, that cause my chest to tighten.

Spoken by the psychiatrist,
Noted down by me,
(In case we need them as evidence, always fortifying our arsenal of information in readiness for the next battle)
My youngest is living with the legacy of...

"Multiple traumatic experiences in school"

Do not misunderstand.
This is not news.
I have fought the battle for recognition, validation and acknowledgement long, and hard.
But seeing it in black and white somehow has a profound impact.

I have often heard motherhood described as
'Having your heart walking around outside your body.'

This for me is true.
What you don't hear so much of,
Is how it feels to have your heart crushed,
Bruised and beaten down.
Again
And
Again.
Right in front of you,

And in a place the authorities insist they must be.
They simply don't see,

You're forced to look on as your very heart is
Belittled,
Bullied and crushed
Until it doesn't know who it is,
Or how to be,
And wants to die.

But you cannot cry.

Because you are the glue,
You have to fix it,
To find a way,
To fight,
To make it ok.

So here I am.
In the calm after the storm (according to the Professionals!)
Sitting in my kitchen.

Neither of my children now in school,
But living with it's legacy
As we find a way to move forward
Slowly
Gently,

Beyond the pain.

We start again.

Building hope,
Embracing this new way of being.

Seeing them grow,

But it's slow.

Very,

Slow.

And in the moments of peace,
Of stillness
And quiet

I allow myself to feel the pain.

To own it.

To name it.

Parental trauma.

Yet even as I do, I question it.
And myself.
Hidden away on a very high shelf,
Feelings on hold,
To survive
Whilst I fought to secure the support
For my children
To thrive.

I listen to the birdsong outside my window,
Watch the laundry dancing in the breeze
I breath In
And out.

The notes are there on the page.
But I'm not ready to feel them yet.
Because despite the 'professionals' opinion "You're past the worst of the storm"
I know there could be more to come.
Hyper-vigilance became a part of me,
Somewhere along the way.

And for a while yet It's here to stay.

Another meeting next week,
Because despite the lull, the "calm"
"Multiple traumatic experiences" don't just vanish.

I must now arm myself
For the next fight.
It is a constant process
That will take you closest
That you've ever been
To the edge.

My phone lights up with a message...
My youngest, with a plea, and a link
To buy a chicken coop no less!

And I smile.

Despite the "multiple traumatic experiences"
Which left us housebound for years.
We are still standing.

Just.

And learning about chickens, And finding our way.

My trauma must wait

For another
Day.

My daughter of seasons

Hair cascading over her shoulders
Tousled ringlets of
Muted gold and amber,
Subtle, amber, auburn tones..
Mirroring nature's autumnal beauty.

Eyes wide with wonder,
Drinking in the crisp November morning
Relishing the crunch of leaves underfoot
And marvelling at the stoic seagull
Battling against the autumnal winds
Voicing its avian thoughts...
What wizardry is this?

Always seeing what others miss
The shape of the branch
The pattern in the clouds
The mushrooms dotted neath the trees
As her thoughts zig-zag like the darting starlings that catch her eye.

Wrapped up warm against the chill
She will sometimes venture out
But for the most part

This is her season of rest.

She nests

Enveloped by the reassuring warmth of an oversized sweater,

flickering festive lights

And the sweet smell of gingerbread

She used to fight it

Valiant determination to 'soldier on'

Keep up the 'normal' and deny her earth soul's need to

hibernate

Create

a space to rest.

But now she is wiser

And rather than resenting,

Fearing,

how her body asks for calm

She has learned to wrap

Herself in blankets

Of self-compassion.

She'll read and she'll write

And try not to fight

Her need to rest.

Instead, there are other ways to fill her days

With lessons

And music
With art and with plans
Of adventures
Upon which she is yet to embark
Destined to make her mark on this world.
My beautiful girl.

And some days the darkness
And cold
Are too much
Icicles of uncertainty
The chill of self-doubt
Muted
And still
We wait
For the spring
Taking heart

In the knowledge
That sure as the seasons turn and the sun rises
So too, shall she.

And when the darkness fades snow and ice thawing
Vibrant green buds emerge as spring unfurls and stretches,
the days, as though just for her
My daughter of seasons

Hopes shooting upwards

Tendrils reach to the blue skies

Vibrance and aspiration now bear fruition

As she turns her face towards the sun

Her season has come.

And I haven't made the crumble

Each day, when I open my eyes,
for a brief moment my heart lurches.
And that's before the coffee.

Hyper-vigilance is not a friendly wake up call.
Immediately my brain is listing in front of me everything that needs to be done,
by what time, for whom
and specifically how.

My husband, who speaks a physical love language,
is disappointed when I cannot relax into an embrace.
Already on my aching feet and stumbling towards the bathroom.

He doesn't hide it well.

My inner critic notes this and puts it on a separate tab so I can chastise myself for not meeting his needs a little later, when a window opens up.

Meanwhile on a drop down tab there's the to do today list, the one of mundane, but incredibly important tasks.

The ones that mean home feels safe.

The right clothes,
Towels
Toiletries...don't run out.
Safe toiletries are pivotal.
The right pj's washed and ready.
The laundry washed and hung separately.
And placed on the chair, not the bed, when clean and dry.

The weighted cutlery accessible.
The right brand of cereal.
Communal areas tidy…
too much clutter brings a wave of overwhelm that could derail the day.
Water bottles washed,
rinsed and re-filled for both.
Reminders to drink.
She'll forget and get poorly.
Must remember to remind her.
The in car circulation button on
(lest we be contaminated by school children air)
Volume on an even number.
Is there enough petrol?

And just for good measure a third tab now starts playing, the 'have you made that appointment?' one.

The dentist...its been way too long, bad mother.

Book it, you'll have to prep them though.

The immunisation..Still one outstanding, need to chase that specialist phobia clinic .
GP won't accommodate.

Complaint about ableist GP, and second opinion for the cardiology referral.
Email practice manager, and put in repeat prescription

Physio..isn't that due?

CAMHS review..crap that's this week

And the EHCP has still not been finalised.
Must leave another message, or email line manager.

And somehow, with the mental noise of these tabs playing simultaneously,
demanding my attention,
I've made breakfast and supported two young people to begin their day.

By lunchtime, ongoing support needs have been met, dogs walked, shopping bought, meals planned, floors hoovered, emails sent, coffee consumed.

And then I hit the wall.

AND I HAVEN'T MADE THE APPLE CRUMBLE!

There are moments when I feel quite literally like I can stand no more.

I sit on my bed and allow myself a moment to cry from the sheer frustration of the exhaustion I feel. The injustice of it all. Why can't I just celebrate and enjoy the changes? We've come so far.

I'm embracing the new routines, and I'm beyond thrilled to see my children stepping back into the world from a place of authenticity and surrounded by love and support.

And...

I'm burnt out.

My body feels so incredibly heavy.

Because whilst we hauled up When they shut down,
And they rested from a place of no demands,
Of comfort,
And softness.

I continued.

Supporting,
Advocating,
Living on the edge, on the verge ,
Always
of a potential collapse or explosion.

Living on pause waiting for the email response you long for.

Stealing yourself to reply with the gusto required.

The tears I cry are of being so very tired of fighting and doing, without drawing breath.
My lead like limbs cannot even lift themselves to brush my tangled hair.

Now I sit on the floor,
In the corner of my bedroom (corners are somehow very comforting)
and quietly sob
In my underwear.
After months, years even,
of trauma ,
Of fighting the system,
Of complaints,
Of watching my children endure mental health crisis with little

to no professional support,
Of surviving minute to minute
Of living through lockdown which both preceded and outran Covid.
Of isolation.
Of advocating, unheard for your child's needs
Of enduring judgement and blame...

When changes come,
like tiny green shoots of hope
That flourish under your loving care ,
And the sunlight streams through the windows as you drive your once housebound child to ride horses and feed goats...and your daughter astonishes you daily with her humour, her passion, her vision...

Your internal critic admonishes you for your lack of energy and celebratory vigour.
And another app pings.

But this one is different.
This one is a picture of your daughter.
Your beautiful,
Brave,
Sensitive daughter.

Wise beyond her years she has forwarded to you the wise

words of another, words she instinctively knew you needed to hear.

And in that moment, I am reminded that I do not have to do it all at once.

It's OK if there are dishes in the sink, My children are fed.
It's OK if I need to order take out more often than is socially acceptable.
Screw socially acceptable.

As a Neuro-spicy family our needs are many,
And mostly met by one.
This will in time change, as so many other wonderful things have.
But for now, hands need to be held as they take brave steps forward.

I smile.
I breath.
I stand.
I dress.
(I look at the hairbrush..but let's not go there)

And whilst the list continue to scroll, draining my battery like a background app left running on your phone,
I find respite in the realisation that I can choose which balls to

drop.
Or to put down, just for a while.
I smile
Again.

The laughter of my youngest carries in through the kitchen window, he's busy cuddling his chickens on a video call to a friend.

My daughter peeps over the cover of one of her many beloved books, immersed in her literary world she is nourished and calm, joined on the arm of her chair by her potato mascot (that's another tale)

The dogs run in circles around my toes,
All fluffy ears and cold, wet nose.

And I walk into the kitchen.
Pour myself some tea.
Quiet the list with the radio,
And pick up the huge, shiny apples.
I peel them ,
I smother them in crunchy, stimmy demerara sugar...
And, much to my children,
and husband's delight (his other love language is food)

I begin making apple crumble.

Faded writing worn with time

Today, I removed a sign from the window.
Nothing remarkable there you may say.
Only this was more than a sign.

The cool breeze, refreshing after the days of sweltering heat, caught at the paper sign, it came dancing through the open window lifting the paper as it fluttered and flipped, clung to the glass.
I held my breath as I pulled it free, and placed it on the kitchen table.
The sign was so faded with age and daylight, that the message was now barely visible
But, I could just make out
'All parcels to the side gate please. Thank you'
My heart contracted in my chest, as reading the words I was taken momentarily back to the time I wrote the sign and placed it prominently in the window to catch the attention of any delivery drivers, bringing any parcels, before they knocked on the door.
The door that could not,
Be,
Opened.

It was last summer.
The days were long and littered with emotional landmines,

ready to explode, bringing destruction and tears in their wake.
The catalyst. OCD. Anxiety. It seemed, last summer, as though they'd never be quite free.
My darling child held captive.
The house a fortress, not to be infiltrated by the likes of a well-meaning delivery driver. Shrouded by darkness, curtains closed, windows locked.
As they sat, immersed in an online world, trying to maintain some kind of connection,
With some kind of community.
Seeking 'normal' when life was anything but.
Fans blasting, hot, stale air around our home as we longed to feel the breeze.
And for them,
To be free.

Last summer.

It seems a world away.
Today, I look down at the faded writing, and dare to smile.
We may not yet be free, completely.
But, my darling child sits smiling.
Chatting,
Singing,
Laughing with their online friends.
The windows open wide and the cool breeze dancing joyously through our home.

And I am reminded, that when things feel dark.

And scary,

And futile.

We must hang on.
Wait a while.
Time can do great things.
Bringing solitude, rest and recovery for them.
(Emails, phone-calls and research for me.)
You see,
With the right support and now the love of some chickens,
Once closed windows are now open wide.
And the child
Who was once held captive,
Has stepped out of the darkness
To venture outside.

There was a time

There was a time, not so long ago, when I felt utterly alone.

Surrounded by well meaning people who had literally no concept of what our lives were like. They'd offer platitudes and ask questions I'd already asked myself a million times over.

They'd post insta perfect pictures of their insta perfect families, doing everyday insta perfect things.

They'd offer cliche phrases and share their unwittingly ableist and stereotyped views on my children's 'questionable' neurodivergence and genuinely think they were offering comfort

" But they don't look autistic do they? I mean you'd never know!"

They'd question my child lead, supportive approach as enabling over dependence. They'd talk of self care, and not pouring from an empty f#cking cup.
My cup broke long ago. It cracked in too many places.

The intensity.
The challenge,
Of navigating the rapidly changing seasons of teenage neurodivergent emotions, with impromptu storms of mental illness thrown in, a shower of trauma, and the wreckage and

debris of hopes and plans to wade through.

With a system so flawed that it was as though it was designed to undermine, to infuriate and to crush any parent who was insolent enough to ask for the right support or, heaven forbid, Education for their children.

A system that broke me.

And left me, fighting, flailing and
Alone.
Until one day, after a particularly tumultuous morning, I discovered quite by chance, that there were in fact other families like ours.

Many.

My phone had long been my escape, my nod towards 'self care', but this was the first time I really felt that it could save me.
Literally save me.

The flood of relief and the waves of non judgmental acceptance were overwhelming.

And as I read through the posts and responses on this facebook group, I realised that in a quiet unassuming corner of the Internet, I'd found a place of acceptance, of genuine empathy born from similarly lived experience,

I'd found my community.

And unless you've ever experienced what it means to be totally lost, you'll never fully know what it means to be found.

Validation
Empathy
Acceptance
Identity
I found them all and more.

And armed with this new support, this sense of belonging, of being held in a place of safety, I became bolder.

Louder
Stronger
As I fought for my children.

These friends, whom I've never, and may never meet face to face, they willingly offer comfort in the darker times,
hope and genuine understanding. They celebrate our achievements, things that to others who walk a more black and white path are unremarkable,

Here they are a source of joy and of hope as we soak up the vast array of colours and hues our children paint in their wake. Their humour, their wit and their honesty.

They are not broken, they are the rebels,
And the revolutionaries

We laugh together
We cry together
And in the written words (and with thanks to my phone),
We find solidarity, humour, kindness and love.
And,

We are no longer
Alone.

Just take a different route

One day a week
My child leaves the house
(If the planets align and the voice of doubt is not too loud)
To play
Tennis.

This, is a monumental challenge.
We drive the same route each time.
It is not the fastest or most direct route,
That, I know.
But, it avoids passing the hospital.
For my child,
That is enough.

There is another reason.

You see, I must be the voice of calm
Of reason and reassurance.
They look to me, for strength
To draw courage from my calm demeanour
Like an emotional anchor in times of fear and uncertainty.

Mum is calm, it must be OK,
Even if it's scary for me,
Mum is smiling.

She's got my back.

And to do that,
I must know the route. If I am to be their calm I must arm myself
With the courage of my convictions.
My mind already spent by the time I turn the key,
And start the car.

A ten-minute drive, maybe fifteen,
It's not that far
But,
In order to leave the house,
I will have spent the previous two hours
Ensuring that the many variables that could derail their determination,
Are, in fact,
Not variable.
But predictable and sure.

The right wake-up call
(The dog opens the door!)
Cereal
Time in the bathroom
The right products
The right clothes
(Washed in the right detergent, labels removed…of course)

The right trainers
And drink cup
And snack.
The right music
Car windows closed.
And, with all of the above in place,
They can (sometimes) face
Tennis.
And I understand the need
For everything to be 'just so'
In order to go.

But today I saw a road closure sign.
Our normal route
Will not be an option this week.
And I realise that the panic I feel
Is not only for my child.
But also, for me.

My husband stares
Perplexed
Vexed.
Just take a different route!
And proceeds to regale me with a multitude of options,
Faster, more efficient
(But they go past the hospital)
Misses all the traffic

(But I can't see it in my head...don't know where to begin)
He's still talking.
I'm taking
Nothing
In.

And we both know
That if I'm to go
I will need to study maps,
Find my own way,
(Keeping the detour as close as possible to our normal route.)
Rehearse it well,
Before the day.

But right now, I can't think how.
Feeling small,
And fragile,
And not at all like an anchor at all
More a chaotic fishing net,
With holes,
And rips at the seams.

It seems to me I'm deficient
Incompetent.
Foolish.
Sobbing,
I berate myself

Why can't I just take a different route?

But I refuse to hate myself
And through the tears,
I try to offer myself the same compassion I would to my child.

Neurodiversity is not a flaw
A difference yes,
A beautiful,
Creative,
Vibrant
Difference,
But not a flaw.

The tears are replaced
With a sombre acceptance.
A heaviness
Inside.

I can't hide, this part of me any longer,
The vulnerable me,
Who needs predictability
To feel stronger,
And be the anchor for our child.

But he can't speak of it.

(That's not who he married.)
It remains unsaid.
Hangs in the air.

Just out of reach.

We both know
I'll make my own plan,
Find my own way,
And much to his frustration
It won't be the quick route
He told me today.

I'll be my child's anchor
Get to tennis
(If they can, if the planets align
And the toast is just right!)
And we won't fight,
My husband and I,
Just feel a sadness that I must
Tackle this challenge in spite of him,
Rather than with his help,
Support.
He ought to understand,
Accept
By now.

And so somehow

We carry on,

With day-to-day life...

And I hope that one day

He'll see,

That I am different

But not less.

And I am still…

His wife.

The gap

I saw you today.
I raised my arms to sweep my hair into a messy bun,
And your eyes darted to my unshaven underarms.
You scowled.
You judged me then;
I saw it in your eyes.
I became less to you.
In that brief moment.
You didn't see that I've not had an uninterrupted bath for months and rarely have time to shower.
You saw that I'd let myself go.

Not that I've been forced to let go of unattainable ideals.
And try to embrace the me I can be.

Rather than the 'old me' you so clearly long for,
And miss.
I'm not her anymore, she got lost along the way.

I saw you today
Deny our child's gender and their neurotype all in one sentence.
To a stranger.
In their presence.
Rather than riding out your own discomfort, and validating our

child's identity.
And I heard you, when they challenged you.
Advocating for themselves,
With you, their father.
You
Dismissed them.
And in that moment,
You widened the gap between us.

I saw you today
Frowning.
Huffing and puffing your impatience at the accommodations needed by our daughter.
In order to travel, she can't do so on the motorway,
Needs an escape route in case panic sets in.
Needs a scenic journey to get from A to B.
Without judgement.
Or comment.
But comment you did; your way was quicker.
Never mind the fear and discomfort it would've caused.
It would've been quicker your way.
That made her feel less.

And the gap widened further.

I saw you;
I heard you

Dismiss and gaslight me for requesting branded, 'safe' foods for our children.
Especially whilst away from home,
With everything different,
Safe, samey foods are so needed.
But the fridge is stuffed to the brim with cheaper, unbranded foods,
A false economy as they will not be eaten.
And in doing this, in yet another way, you demonstrated that our children's needs are not truly seen.

And the gap widened further.

I saw you bristle as your misgendering was corrected,
Not an acknowledgement of thanks, for the help in remembering,
But a petulant, overly exuberant apology,
To incite guilt on the part of the speaker,
For the personal attack they've subjected you to,
By asking that you call your child by their pronouns.
You made it a problem, where there just needn't be one.

And the gap widened further.

I tread on eggshells around you,
Feel a clenching in my chest
When I need to voice an accommodation

That our children need at home,

When I know how you'll react.

Irritation at the personal inconvenience.

Resignation

But rarely the authentic acceptance I long for in you,
In my partner, the father of my children.
I wish so hard for you to meet us where we are.
To embrace the vibrant colours of neurodiversity
Rather than seeing them as a blanket of muted grey,
suffocating your ideals.

It is so incredibly hard to practise self-compassion,
 And embrace the me I've come to know.
When you see this me as less.
Less, than the masked version,
The all seeing, smiling, doing me.
And as I let my guard down and try to live authentically.
I'm 'snappy' and 'unapproachable'
Apparently...

So, the gap widens further.

And I keep hoping that somehow,

we'll find a way to bridge it,
because as it stands,
sometimes I'm lonelier when I'm with you,
Than when I'm alone.

And I know you're unhappy.

And I know you feel low.

But,
Please know
I've tried to help you understand, with blogs and books and posts.
But instead, you chose escapism and denial.
Spending your time doom scrolling social media
And watching random videos with random content
Filling time, and waiting for your nice 'normal' family to return.

Only we aren't going back, for those years nearly broke us.
The smiles and laughter were plastic, were shiny, and fake.
We must keep moving forwards, towards authenticity,
Away from the avatars we created, we must leave them behind,
To find
Ourselves.

If we are to find our way back to each other,

To bridge the gap that looms ever wider,
I ask this.

I ask that you hear me,
You hear us.
And you see us as we are.

That you learn and embrace the adjustments we need,
See us as strong,
Know we're doing our best?
And accept that our differences
Don't mean that we're less?
Please.
Can you do that?

Because,

If you can,

And if you will,

Maybe there's a chance of bridging the gap,

Still.

I didn't see you there

My dearest love
I'm so very sorry,
It took so many years
of you wrestling with fears,
And doubt and pain
Denying yourself
The right to be free
Authenticity

So, I say again, I'm sorry.
With hindsight - regret
How on earth did I miss it?
You were silently screaming
Mask shiny and gleaming

Performance from a cage
(A bright West End stage)
For years.
And you loved it
That's true,
And you lit up the room
Gliding and leaping
Gracefully keeping,
the audience entranced
As you danced

(Holding back tears)
As you danced
(Anxious for years)
Presented with trophies
And so many shows
The teacher's award,
(The embodiment of..)
"The Show Must Go On"

Until the smile was gone...

Gone.

The cracks started to show
At first it was slow
But in the space of mere months
Lost your light,
Lost your shine
A rapid decline
"She's fine here in school,
Always sticks to the rules..."
Collapsed on the floor
"I can't take any more"

My love I'm so sorry
That it took you to break
How on earth will I ever make,

The lost years up to you?

And part of you wondered
And part of you knew

But I'd silenced your questions
Thought it couldn't be true

Not you.

My love I'm so sorry.

It took someone else
(It should have been me- blinded by stereotypes
I just couldn't see)
A professional saw you
Saw through you
The true you
My love

The true you
My love

She asked about autism
And ADHD
Little did I know
Those words they would save you

They found you,
And freed you

My love

I'm so sorry
I didn't know better
Do better
By you.
You knew.
The relief, validation
That came with recognition
And a journey began
And you started to plan!

And tiny, then growing
Your flame, embers glowing

With knowledge,
Came identity
Embracing who
You were meant to be
My love
I'm so sorry
It took so very long.

For me to hear the lyrics,
Beyond the melody
Of your song.

For so long
you were muted
Unacknowledged
Surviving
An autistic young woman
Now growing
Now thriving

Embracing
Understanding
Traits you felt were your flaws
Self-compassion
And impassioned
To break through those doors

Shedding the mask that broke you apart
And the toll that it took
On your head
And your heart

Before we saw through
Saw you with clear eyes,
Past autism myths

and professional's lies.

My love.

I'm so sorry.

That it took so long.

I didn't see you,

You had to be so strong

A journey it's been

And we've all come so far

And now we behold you

A phoenix,

The true you

Rising from the embers

Of what you endured

Moving on

Striding forward

Authentic and

Self-assured.

♡

Shepherds pie and scrambled eggs

My dearest love
You made shepherd's pie.

You peeled, chopped, stirred and fried.
You mashed, you topped with cheese.
You did all this whilst listening to the radio and dancing along.
You have a new song.
A glorious new song.
You presented your dish with a flair and stood smiling proud and tall,
Had climbed that impossible wall.

Only a few short months ago
even leaving the solace of your room was too much.
Couldn't bear to venture into the kitchen let alone cook.
Hid in a book.
I tried your favourites but knew, you were still unsteady
You weren't ready.

But yesterday you made eggs for breakfast, for me, and tea
And today you made shepherd's pie,
Whilst I weathered a storm upstairs
You were there, mashing it,
Smashing it.
A brighter you so vibrant

That time had not been wasted

And that pie, my love, your very own, the best I've ever tasted.

♥ ♥ ♥

Anecdotes from Neurodivergent family life…

When Monday sees your child's online science tutor valiantly teaching the structure of the cell, whilst your child sporadically does laps of the room on a Segway with Tics in full flow, shouting "You love to shag sheep!"
Or, my personal favourite...
"Stick a carrot up my a#$e and call me Susan!" EOTAS is never dull.

———

When you type 'y o...' into google and your immediate results are: Yorkshire Pudding Recipes
       Young Minds Crisis Messenger service

———

When your child doesn't sleep until midnight then starts calling at 3.30am.
By 5.30am (and having been called to sleep negotiations - no you can't have your Nintendo switch - at 10-minute intervals) you give up and go downstairs. By 7am they have moved the furniture, are riding a Segway, wearing only pants and slipper boots, playing guitar and singing Feliz Navidad in a very animated fashion. That's ADHD right there!

———

Whilst attempting to cut a slice of frozen cheesecake..
Me: you could just wait ten minutes and try again?

Daughter: I think not. I am the embodiment of determination.

Herculean strength come to me! Be mine!

See!

(Walks away with frozen cheesecake)

Whilst walking the dogs, daughter's dog darts onto the nearest drive, in pursuit of a cat.

Me: "Ned, no come away"

Daughter: "Why must he? What's so very wrong with him making new friends?"

Me: "Nothing darling, but not on other people's property"

Daughter: " He is a nomadic being, thus he believes that no one has ownership of the land."

With my flowing hair, long dress and sandals…I feel kinda like Jesus today. But without the beard.

YOU ABSOLUTE VAGINA

YP in online physics class.

"I need to tell you a joke right now.

A lady at the bank asked me to check her balance,

So, I pushed her over…moving swiftly on"

YP, upon seeing an 80s hair do on TV: Ooh interesting, that's how I want my hair!

Me: That's called a mullet

YP: Yes, I'll have my hair in a mullet, it looks good and I can hit people with it.

Pause

Oh wait, that's a mallet!

Life in 3D

A light bulb moment.
An epiphany.
Not me.

More a dawning realisation, as I watched my beautiful
daughter emerge from her cocoon of self-doubt and spread
her wings, radiant with all the hues of neurodiversity.
I saw those colours and knew some of them as my own.
Not alone,
in living with a mask for so long.
So many strong,
women.
Neurodivergent and incognito,
They did not know.
Or let it show.
And now, they are sleuths
Piecing together clues, from childhood and youth,
And finding that they have many
Moments where they utter
How did I not see?
I thought it was just me!

Disordered eating, and tears about school,
The mystery of friendship and it all,
Falls.

Into place.

And I face my younger self

with wretched, aching heart

She was lost and broken

But did not fall apart...

yet.

Instead, she painted on a smile, entertaining far too many men

Craving affection, admiration

In dangerous places once again.

To look.

To be.

To see.

So, leap forward to today,

All the things I find so hard

That come easily to others,

Whilst I'm there, wondering

Why can't I?

What is wrong with me? Who on earth...

am I?

Could there be a valid reason,

I've always felt so square?

Trying to fit society's circular hole?

Playing a role.

A woman once capable and respected.

I can't keep up that image now,

As I struggle to figure out where she ends...
And I begin.
But unmasking feels too scary
So much built on who I've played.
With so much kept inside,
Must hide,
behind the facade
Keep guard
of my fragility

My quirks
Or are they 'traits'?
I can't bring myself to look, not fully.
I can wait.

For my family, holding space, face
Holding it together
But my children, they see through me
See the true me.

Going through the motions
Though no more muted grey,
Colours leaking, can't quite be contained...
And each day reading memes, and posts
And articles that scream at me
Neurodiversity!
Hello!

Don't just let this go?

So many others,
relatable stories and clues.
It's not just you.
No one knew!

And this realisation,
new knowledge that I've found
Brings self-compassion,
Connection,
Empathy
And common ground.
A new dimension to my mothering
And to being
Me.

So no,
no light bulb moment here.
But a gradual understanding
Of why I've been so tired all these years!
And in my children,
I see diversity, difference,
Individual experience.
I don't have to fit a criteria?
You mean I'm not actually inferior?
Afterall.

For so long, so many facets that I've shut away,
Feeling less of a woman because I just don't see things that way?

You mean that's ok?

A dawning realisation brings freedom
Brings connection
To a tribe of others
Daughters
Mothers

Relief,
Slow burning self-belief
Begins.

And sadness,
(That in time I'll face,
when I feel strong enough.)
Grief for the woman struggling through
Clutching to the mask,
Scared to ask
Does anyone else feel this way?
Whilst sinking.

Affirmation, the life buoy of self-identity,
You see
It's OK not to have a diagnosis
This is about me!
Not a tick box exercise I'm not a list of
Traits.

It's not too late
To realise
Seeing with now open eyes.
(still not sure what it means right now)
 But
Authenticity
And letting my colours leak
Not smothered, grey and bleak.

No,
I am not an imposter
I'm real
I'm here
I haven't lost
Her.

Seeing myself as though through those paper glasses
Red and blue,
and other hues

Life no longer as a stifled whisper.
Or saccharine smile,
singing to the harmony
Dictated by society.

No, after all these years I'm me,
But now
In 3D.

♥

Oranges

We have never voiced it, never said it out loud.

But I have a sneaking suspicion that my husband knows I am autistic as much as I do.

And that it's ok.

Because he still buys my oranges, which is not a simple task.

You see I can only eat the ones shaped like the Millennium Falcon, slightly squashed in shape.

But not the very spherical death star.

I can't eat those; they sit in the fruit bowl until they crawl to the bin themselves! So, buying oranges takes him some time as he holds up the nets of sweet fruit to see which space craft they resemble most closely…

before bringing them home to me. 🖤

Twilight Walk

Inside, looking out,

Missing out.

The world,

Just outside the window.

No,

Can't go.

Full of danger

Dread.

Instead,

Stay inside.

Hide.

Away,

Until today.

Some talk of OCD as a monster

To beat

Or shrink.

But,

It makes them sad

To think of it

As 'bad'

Empathy so strong

Wrong

To demonise

Vilify

Instead, how about we

Try.

Try to teach OCD

To take a break

Make

Him see,

And feel,

The danger isn't

Real.

OCD saw the hurt

The fear

The pain

It said never again..

Never again.

And it saw danger everywhere

There,

In the garden In the street

Can't meet...

Anyone.

That's how it begun

To grow too big,

Too much,

Can't hold,

Can't touch,

Anyone

Anything.

And now

It's time to take it back

Life

Freedom

The world outside the window.

It needs to know

OCD,

To see,

It can take a break

A holiday

Kept watch for too long

Danger,

Fear,

Too strong.

For years.

Years.

It simply got

The wrong end of the stick

Thought staying inside

Would

Fix

It.

But no.

It's time to go

Outside.

Now.

This night.

In the waning light

Orange, pink sky.

Let's try...

Bird song

Breeze

Spring flowers

Green trees

Happy dog

Wagging tail

Sparrows

Tulips

Baby snail

You see OCD!

It's not so bad!

Think you'll be glad

To take a back seat?

It's time,
We meet,
Face to face,

As I take back this place
My home
My street
My garden
My mind.
Free will.

Still,
OCD may always be there In part
Just no longer
In control
Of their heart,
Or their head.

Instead,
Put in a pocket,
Along for the ride
No longer a prisoner
No staying inside.

A dog walk today
Pink cheeked
Standing tall.

Ventured out

In the evening

Through the grass

Saw it all

Before them.

Waiting for them

Beyond the window...

Watching

(With bated breath)

As off...

They...

Go...

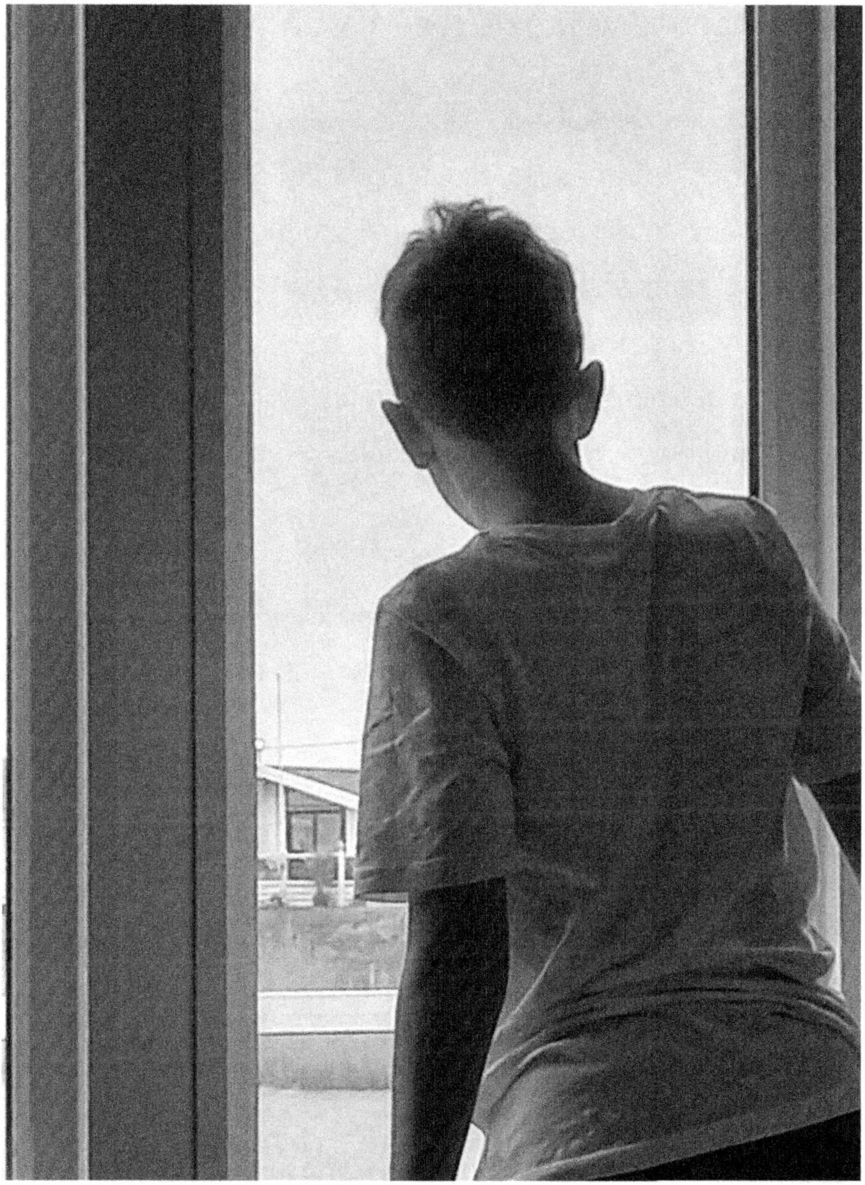

Hope wrapped with a ribbon

The candle light flickers, dancing, to the soothing, melodic tones of the Christmas Carol playing softly on the radio.
The dogs lay on my feet, their weight grounding and comforting as they snore contentedly. I feel a heart beating against my skin. And smile.
The glass of Sherry, sits now half empty among the pile of ribbons and bows as though intentionally festooned for the occasion.
I yawn (well it is 1am). And smile.
I take another pair of socks and inside it I place a peppermint candy cane and a chocolate Santa wrapped in brightly coloured foil.
I fold the paper neatly over and secure with tape, finishing with a dark green ribbon. And a label.
I add this parcel to the pile of others. Twelve in total, for twelve members of staff. And another, slightly bigger pile of oddly shaped parcels, precariously balanced but lovingly wrapped. A pile of gifts containing footballs, a yoga ball, a mirror, a cardboard tunnel and a garden herb pick and mix! These are not gifts for classmates , but for the hens, the goats, the ferrets and the horses! In fact every animal has to have a gift, and to my wonder and surprise, so too must every member of staff. So as the clock ticks on, and the dogs gently snore, I gladly wrap these gifts. Doing so is, in itself, a gift I never imagined possible.

I sip my Sherry.

And run my fingers over the satin ribbon.

Only a few months ago, my child had been imprisoned by their trauma, their anxiety and these four walls.

This table, this chair ,

this kitchen had been my world.

The living room theirs, a gaming screen and headset their only window...their only light. Wintering,

hibernating,

Licking our wounds

And waiting for the spring.

Which came in time,

Heralding change,

Warmth,

And light.

The daffodils had bloomed in our little garden, their golden heads haphazardly nodding, dancing,

Celebrating.

For through one (of the many) groups for families like ours, we had heard tell of a place that gave us a glimmer of hope.

We found this place of nature, and straw

and mud.

Of patience,

of kindness and of growth.

And yet it hadn't been simple, it hadn't been smooth. Trauma doesn't stay at home in a neat little box,
But rather it had travelled with my child,
ready to cast doubt and suspicion over these new people and this place.
It was risky.
It took great courage, strength and trust.
Trauma is a complex companion. Reminders, triggers, lurking in the bushes Ready to sabotage in its attempt to preserve, and prevent more pain.
But we had welcomed him and named him, Trauma, this part of my child.
And in doing so,
by offering compassion and validation,
he somehow became smaller whilst my child, They grew.
Red cheeks, aching bones, dishevelled hair and muddy boots.
The muddy boots,
And the smile.

Slowly, very slowly they had learned to trust. These adults didn't punish!
Didn't berate their energy, their speed of light thinking, or belittle their fears.

Here, among the pigs, from the branches of the trees (with a safety harness!) and around the crackling camp fire, was a place to grow.

The radio plays another familiar Carol,
and the dog wags his tail, thumping gently against my leg,
As though reading my mind from the depths of his peaceful slumber. I smile and finish my Sherry.
The last gift is wrapped.
I place it on the teetering pile, and put away the tape and ribbon.
I blow out the candle and turn off the radio.

Time for bed.

We are ready for the last day of term,

And we will wait with anticipation for the New Year, For the inevitable hiccups,
the peaks and the troughs.

We, like so many others, have no picture or map for our destination.
We are still finding our way through rocky territory,
But tonight I wrapped gifts for my child to share with adults they have come to trust.
That is enough.
We are on the right track.

They will still carry with them, The 'what came before'

But, laden with presents,
Wearing boots still caked in mud,
Tomorrow they'll waken
And they'll walk through the door.

Now you see me

There was a time,

Not so long ago,

That I knew you couldn't see me,

Not the real me,

Just a shadow of the one before.

Before our lives turned upside down,

And I finally found

Myself.

Hidden way

Beneath a mask.

Not all at once, like a face reveal,

But over time,

The layers peeled

Away.

And as I came to know and meet our children's Needs,

I found reflections of my own,

In the luminescent beauty of their dynamic souls.

I found more than just holes,

Gaps,

Where I should've been.

Found worth in my quirks

And I let them be seen.

By you.

Miscommunication

Frustration

Parallel people

But not side by side,

For so long.

And I'd asked myself, through the torrent of tears,

If you could take the leap,

Bridge the ever-widening gap,

And join me.

Join our children

Authentically.

Then,

As Christmas drew closer

So too

Did we.

I began to see light,

Growth and change

In you.

In us.

Not without setbacks

But you were really trying

And that

Was enough.

It was the small things,

Isn't it always?

That began bridging the gap

Accepting my mad

My wild happy,

And sad

Moods

As I continued to navigate the perilous waters of parenting our wildling pair.

You were there.

Listening

Learning

Caring

With a hug,.

A cup of tea

A new mug (or two, as I'd smashed the last one,

And we knew all too well, this one could share its fate)

And it's turned out

That for us

It wasn't

Too

Late.

The calm before the storm

It's a phrase we often hear, and one to which I closely relate.

The sense of trying desperately to live in the moment, to breath and pause, nurturing hope and patience.

To seize the good times and allow them to energise and replenish, to celebrate positivity and progress in our own individual way.

But what if the storm shadow looms too great? What then?

What if we've become so used to the changes in the air that tell of turbulence and strife that we simply cannot be calm anymore? Hypervigilance has become our way of life and we no longer know another. We have become desensitised to the racing heart and sweaty palms, the heightened senses of smell and sound as we scan constantly for the next trigger , and resulting crescendo of emotion. This is the way it is now.

So we do celebrate the steps forward our children and young people are forging. We see them moving, growing, changing. We laugh with them, root for them and hope with all our hearts that this is the start of something good. All the while terrified that it's not. Because we all know. Boy do we know.

Recovery isn't linear. Help is hard to come by and our systems are beyond broken.

And on those rare occasions we step away from our young ones for that Holy Grail of restorative rest and relaxation...a concert, a massage, a dinner, a nap...we find that in fact the fallout of our absence quickly engulfs the peace we briefly knew.

'YOU weren't here!'

Sometimes shouted, screamed through teeth gritted in fury and fear.

Sometimes yelled without words but through needs and demands, and more needs, and more demands, that must be met 'Now!' to soothe their souls and restore balance to their teetering sense of security.

For we are the constant, the safety net, the anchor that tethers our young ones in this hostile world, inhospitable to our neurokind. Often cruel and with challenges seemingly insurmountable. We guide them , we hold them, we show them. Often whilst we are still honing our own navigational skills inside.

And we drink tea, or coffee, or wine. And our windows of 'calm before the storm' become ever smaller.

Until one day, it hits us. We realise that there is no calm before our storm, because we are in fact, the storm!

Exhilarating, exhausting, energising and beautiful in its own tumultuous way.

We cannot live our lives dreading the turmoil, but instead we must see it. We must welcome it, and envelope it with compassion, guided by our neurokin and fellow storm bringers!

We must yell our own fury and frustration into its roaring winds, and know in time, hand in hand with our young ones, we'll find our way.

Wrapped in blankets of validation and authenticity, we'll rest and recover...

as the wind whistles on and rain lashes at our window panes.

We'll find our own calm, within our storm.

The beach

The car doors open,
Breeze on my face
Hastily freeing the dogs from the car
There they are,
My loves,

Eager to take the leads,
Take the lead,
The roar of the sea,
Or is it my heart?
Racing,
Pounding in my chest
Lest,
I should wake from this dream...

Been here so often,
In my mind,
Seen this moment,
Heard the pebbles crunch beneath my feet

Heat, of the spring sunshine on my face
This place,

Is it real?

For so long we've lived inside four walls
Lockdown never ended for us.
Trust,
And faith took time,
For so very long…
Learning how to be strong
In themselves.

Broken apart
We went back to the start
Safety and sameness,
Building strength from inside.
Hide,
In routine, and four walls.

Dreaming of a day, we may find a way
To step into the light.
We might,
One day,
See the sea again.

Walk hand in hand,
On the sand, or the stones
Not alone,
But together.

Forever it's seemed we have waited,

But now here we are

They're out of the car,

Wind in their hair

They're running

They're there!

My heart overflows
Knows, the journey we've been on
To get where we are.
And the joyous tears fall
All at once,
I can't speak,

Or breathe

Or move.

Can't lose,

This moment.

He reaches for my hand
Tears in his eyes

No words.

Just standing side by side.

Watching our children

Chasing the waves.

Chasing the waves,

Laughing,

Chasing the waves,

Pink cheeked,

Unruly hair,

Barking dogs,

They're there.

They made it.

Out of the house,

Out of the dark,

Not without challenge or tears, hesitation

Talking, supporting,

Partnered contemplation.

A journey much deeper than traffic,
Detours.

It was not mine to drive,
This journey was yours

My loves...

And above...

The gulls loudly calling

To the sea, to the skies,

They're announcing your presence

It's begun,

You've arrived....

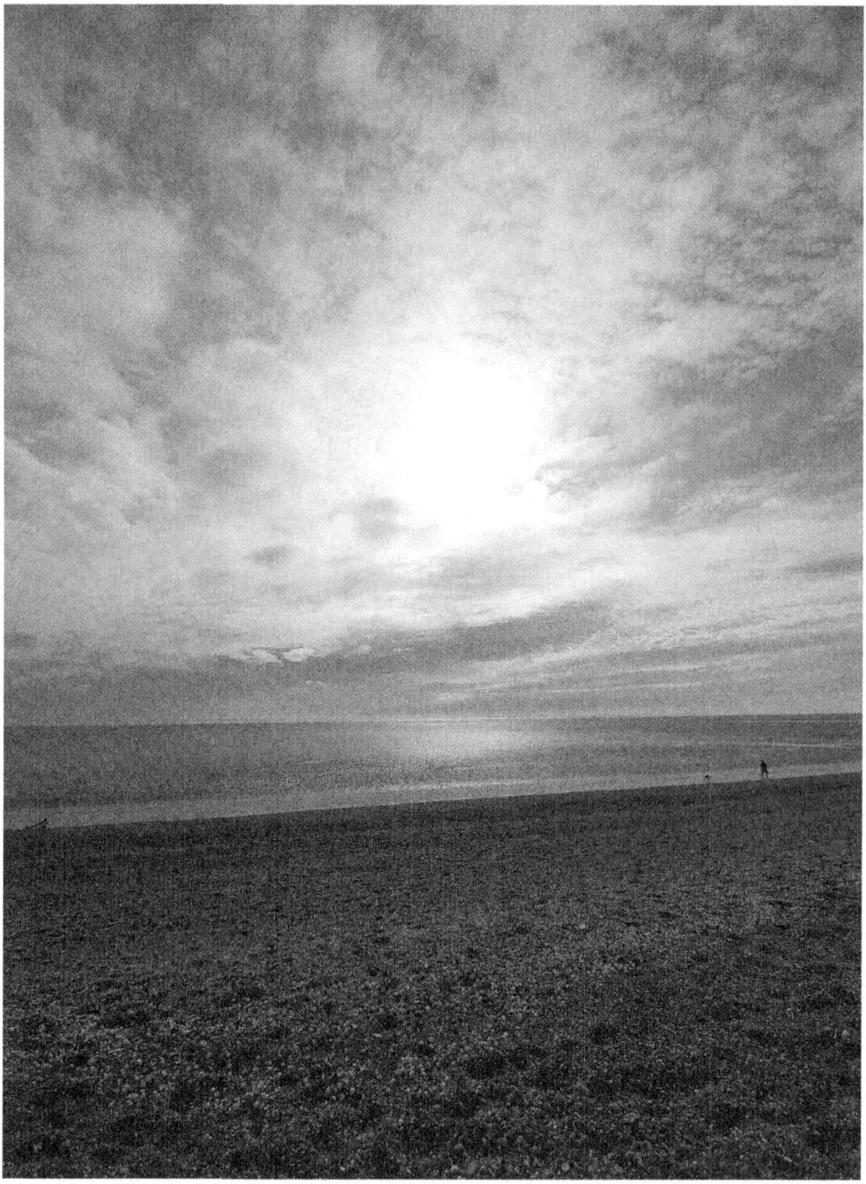

With laughter came light

Today they stood tall,
Smiling.
In the sun.

It had begun...

A few weeks since
When, by chance,
Or was it fate?
We found this place.

Peered through the gate.

Looked beyond
To what might be,

Here.

Not a school
Governed by archaic attitudes
And rules.
No.

A place where the smells
And sights

And sounds

Engulfed them

Wrapped them

In nature,
And in that haven,
They found...

The parts we'd thought broken
Crushed beyond all repair
Were in fact,
To our surprise

Hidden,

But there.

Buried beneath all the hurt,
Disbelief
And sealed in a casket of trauma
And grief.
Their will,
And their spark
Had survived by a thread
And here was a place

That was willing to tread

Gently
And slowly

To move at their pace,

With patience
And kindness
Humour,
And grace.

And in the short time
Since they first trod this path
My child,
My love,
Had found their lost laugh.

Their laughter a signal
A beacon of hope.
Lit by staff so impassioned
To go beyond
"They can cope"

No more talk of endurance
Or hiding your pain.
Support in authenticity

If they could just

Trust

Again.

Today they stood tall,
Smiling,
In the sun,

Laughing over their shoulder

Their journey's begun... (Thank you ADO.)

Black magic

In houses like ours,
And I know there are many,
Turbulence and tears are part of the furniture.
The decor tells tales of spontaneous, trauma induced alterations,
But who needs bathroom fittings anyway?
They'll be replaced one day.

And, the locks on the doors may rarely be opened.
A fortress of safety not to be breached by more than a trusted few.

No one goes in, and no one comes out…

But within these walls, gilded with
Hypervigilance… there lies magic.

True magic.

No house elves here, or strange shaped scars to tell tales of mystical endurance and survival.

The mere fact that we are here and still standing testifies to the strength in our souls.

No the magic here is black.

And furry.

With eyes that see through any mask and straight into your heart.

Each of my wildlings has their own magical companion, and I watch in awe as everyday they spin their web of comfort, of love, of warmth and hope, with a simple wag of the tail or a weighty lean in and snuffle.

Their very scent brings calm.

I have seen the frenzied flailing of flying fists, be calmed by their presence. Their closeness, the feel of their fur between his fingers, the angst melts away as he buries his face in their necks and breathes in the musty yet fresh scent of outdoors and old tennis balls. Of dog food and cheese.

These are the real bringers of magic and mystical calm. Armed with only their loyalty and the purest of loves.

They bring joy and humour, a reason to rise.

Companionship unwavering. Secure, and as solid as his rotund rear as he struts and sometimes lollops on his daily

stroll. Tail quivering, with his endearingly different wagg!
Whilst his counterpart bounds, Red Arrow like, in all directions. Keep up! Follow me! See! The birds, the flowers, the trees, the sticks, the smells, the rain, the spring sunshine. They take it all in, and take us out to be immersed in the wonders of their world.

The scent of fresh lavender the feel of the breeze. And breathe.
When she is adrift, disconnected and scared. They're there.
Laying on, not at her feet.
They ground her, and hold her, their breathing regularing her own as she calms to the rhythmic snores of their soothing slumber.

And laughter, such laughter.
Comedians they are, from afar you'd be forgiven for thinking they're dogs.
Just dogs.

But no, they're the bringers of joy in our home. A toy?
A squeaky toy?
No thank you a sock will suffice (fresh off the foot is preferred)
Or an egg box - now there's the real therapy!
His pure unadulterated joy as he tears it to shreds, tail furiously wagging as though to extinguish an invisible flame. And excitement so authentic and raw it's contagious, as he tosses

back his head and shakes out his black mane before resuming the important task at hand.

Understand though, that it is not only my loves who are calmed when they're near. These magical souls just know when they're needed

And always deliver an appreciative wagg (I'm happy to see you)

Or kiss.

This, is love.

Here in this house, they are cherished with such ferocity, such intensity and gratitude.

Their magic heals and restores me. When I crumple under the weight of holding up the fortress roof, they console and comfort. Instinctively seeking me out with kisses.

Strengthening my resolve. I bury my face in their fur and at their invitation, breathe them in. And then, fuelled by their love, I pick up the slack and carry on. With two magical souls at my heels.

And when the sun shines, and the seasons allow, sometimes now, we do venture out. Together.

A little further.

And as we do, we rejoice in their excitement as they race and frolic on the beach, in the sea, "don't eat the seaweed!"

Leaving pawprints alongside

footprint, entangled and as one.

Family.

Real,

Authentic

Pure.

And I know one thing for sure.

No one goes in and we sometimes come out…

But within these walls, gilded with hypervigilance…

There

Lies

Magic.

These are the boots

These are the tracksuits
That dry on the line,
Dancing in the breeze, triumphantly ,
Defiantly,
Decorated with stubborn stains of mud and dirt,
And a sizeable hole with a tale to tell,
Of a child who at one time could not leave the safety of their room,
But now rips their trousers as they scramble through the branches of the towering oak tree… as they look up to the sky.

These are the boots
That took those first steps.
Out of the door,
The car,
Through the gate.
So long he'd been barefoot,
With no need for shoes.
Before spring arrived,
Bringing sunshine and liberation.
Three pairs of boots he's outgrown these last months!
Cause for celebration!
Caked in mud and horse manure, sticks and rocks wedged in the tread,
They tell of days spent mucking out and grooming,

Campfires and company.
They sit by the door awaiting the next adventure… now they've a reason to get out of bed.

This is the sunhat,
A simple black cap,
Into which he'll tuck his hair
(not so long ago shaven in a moment of pain)
Now grown out into long tousled blonde curls, the peak shielding his eyes but he'll still come home sunkissed and golden.
Pink cheeked, sweaty brow.
For now,
He spends all day outside!

No longer a prisoner,
No need for a screen
Behind which to hide.

This is the chair
Sitting vacant and still.
The room is silent, no bleeping games (not until later)
This room which was his whole world.
For so long.
Lessons, meals, gaming
And connection…

Now stands empty as the silence celebrates in deafening song…

He is not here!

He's outside running wild with the wind in his hair and the rain or the sun or the snow on his skin.
He's re-writing his story,
Found a place to begin.

This is the sister…
With her own weight to carry,
Her own struggles and triumphs
Patiently standing by through his seemingly never ending lockdown.
Waiting.
Listening.

And finding creative, imaginative ways to carry on and move forwards.
Whilst her sibling
Stayed
Stuck.

She now rejoices in the ways things have changed,
The open windows,
The freedom

The birdsong brings elation…

Aboard a long delayed train
As it now leaves the station

This is the father,
For so long at arms length.
Barriers forged by anxiety kept him that way,
Treading on egg shells
OCD brought such fear
Wave from a distance, lest he derail the day.

Now his laughter, visceral and hearty, fills the house
Of an evening as they sit.
Father and son,
Side by side,
Sharing their joy at irreverent humour.

These moments of connection,
Are his tangible proof
That whilst his trauma and illness has come at great cost,
With love at the foundation
All
Was
Not
Lost.

And.

This is the mother
She's still holding her breath
Scared to believe in the changes she sees,
After years of fighting
Brought them all to their knees.
But she's slowly beginning to let her guard down.
With time
And patience

With each passing day
As her daughter stands tall,
And her husband is laughing
And her son at farm school (yes! At school!)

She is beginning to breath
And believe

Things can change

This is the young adult
No more a child.
He stands taller than her now,
His broad shoulders sit just above her own.
Hair unruly and wild
And as he smiles cheekily down at her,

She sees the cogs turning behind his eyes.

Always up to mischief,

Loving dark humour,

Revelling in surprising, another

And, for the most part he's happier

Than in years past,

He now sees a way forward

As too does his mother.

This is the story.

Messy, true and real.

Peppered with hypervigilance,

And trauma

(conflicted sensory needs

… for extra spice)

We're here,

We're together

And beginning to heal.

Authentically us

Sometimes, when the path ahead feels uncertain,
We must pause to catch our breath and look back.
To see how far we've come.
Together.
To name and own our triumphs, however small.
And to see that through it all,
We're still here.

Neither of us are the people we were a few years ago.
We fell in love with different versions of each other, not better, not worse, just different.

Times were simpler then, or so it appeared on the surface.
But beneath the calm facade I'd been frantically treading water,
for a long,
Long,
Time.
I just didn't know it ,
Know how to name it,
Back then.

Internalised, kept inside, the feelings of inadequacy.

Buried deep, as we carried on with our relatively 'normal' life.
A relatively 'normal' husband and wife.

Until little by little the landscape of our lives began to change.

School became a battle field, our children, fighting valiantly for far too long.
We watched them fade before our eyes,
and we were scared.

We found ourselves in uncharted territory.
Me, on the front line wiping tears, holding them as they wept with battle fatigue, and you, desperate to help , to fight alongside me, but stopped in your tracks by the strange and unfamiliar weapons and approaches that were really needed.

Tough love, and pushing through were the plans taught to you.
But in this fight they were powerless and did more harm than good.

They should,
go to school.

But
They
Can't.

And so
It began.

As the war raged on we won some victories, diagnoses giving validation to our two, and a whole new direction to explore.

But more,
was to come.

The burnout bomb hit hard and cruel
Affecting each in different ways,
The days, became long and fraught.

And this was no weekend job, a part time fight that could fit in with our life 'before.'
So, I stopped work, to be there, in the trenches, as was needed. Shoulder to shoulder with our children as they fought on, valiantly, against those inner demons.

And you, my love, made that happen.
You worked long and hard,
To provide the sustenance needed by your troops.

But it meant that we lead quite separate realities, for a time.
I watched you going off to work, and as I bolted the gate behind you I sometimes wept with envy at the thought of the fresh challenges that were to come that day.

At the same time thankful that your leaving meant that I could stay.

It is no wonder we were changed. War leaves scars that can't be seen.
And,
some that can.
I am different,
An unexpected side story being the recognition of my own neurodivergence along the way.

Feeling for so long an imposter, not a real woman, let alone wife,
it's taken time to see,
me.

To realise that so many sources of tension, anger and upset, were because I hadn't understood myself yet, or the message I sent out. You, trying to read my face, whilst what I felt was not reflected there.

You, trying to reach me when I couldn't reach myself.

Identity eluded me,
Hidden high on a messy shelf.

And yet somehow, through the misunderstandings,

The heated exchanges and the distant days.

We
Stayed
Together.

We learned to share our frustrations, and our fears.
And through the tears,

We emerged stronger.

This is not the end of the story, nor is it the beginning.
But,
Somewhere in between.

We have won the battle but are yet to win the war, we know this will take some time.
Trauma doesn't heal overnight.
Mental health is an ongoing fight.
So time,
 lots of time.

And patience.

And love.

Celebrating the small victories,

And accepting the setbacks,
knowing that they do not define us.

Finding light in humour, and in the beauty of all we hold dear around us.
We will keep moving forward.
Remembering to treat each other with compassion when things get tense.

Authentically us,

With no more pretence. X

Down a long winding lane

A connection unspoken.

Between a horse and boy
That could never be broken.

Nigel was the one,
Took this nervous young rider
Anxious, he couldn't do it
Hiding worries with banter

Onwards and upwards
With support from Louise,
Over jumps, no less
In trot and in
Canter!

And whilst riding he loved and it made him feel free,
He learned oh so much more,
So much more
Do you see?

The magic is in a place
Where you feel you belong
They gave him a locker
And with it his heart's song.

They set him to work, they kept him on track
They knew from the start that he'd keep coming back.

For they saw within him what others had not,
Saw his confidence grow
First a walk, then a trot

Magic indeed as his shoulders grew broad,
And with them his smile,
His mischief and wit
He'd found that he was valued, had a seat at the table,
They laughed at his nerve,
When locked in the stable!

And whilst his woes had not gone,
And some days he'd feel low,
When he walked through the gates
The horses would know.

Real magic you see is right there,
In the knowing.
A feeling, a sense

Have you ever seen magic?
I ask once again
We found it in a place down a long winding lane.

And as shadows grow longer
Summer days turn to fall
We look back
And give thanks
To that dear riding school.

Have you ever seen magic?
Real magic I mean?
Not the stuff of sideshows and charlatans
Of mirrors and lights,
But of horses, hooves and happiness
Found in a place down a long winding lane.

So I'll ask again

Have you ever seen magic?

The magic I speak of is the kind rarely seen.
Born from connection,
From kindness and trust
And taking a chance on a new volunteer

Who at the beginning stood quietly by
And looked on in awe as the horses walked on,

But in time would stand tall
As though meant to be here.

A boy who knew heartache, and sadness too well
But through patience and acceptance
Would come out of his shell.

The day she walked away

Today I barely knew her, was in silent awe
And saw the true her.
The vibrant young woman striding fourth with an air of confidence, or was it defiance?
Her auburn hair falling freely in haphazard ringlets about her shoulders,
And her signature furry boots, a contrast to her floaty, floral dress.
Yes.
The epitome of contradiction,
And authenticity.

Unapologetic for her eclectic style,
Head high,
While,
I looked on.
This strong,
And feisty woman,
Blazing her own trail,
Stepping away from the safety rail,
Towards a new start.

My heart, pounding in my chest
As across the crowded lecture theatre,
I hear her.

I hear her voice,
Her wisdom,

Her passion

Ignited,
Delighted,
To have the floor to share and draw her own conclusions,
Articulate analysis
Of the poem on the slide.

This woman will no longer hide.

I walk behind her,
In her wake,
As she strides
Towards her next chapter.

English Literature, at university.
Today a visit, a glimpse of what could soon to be.
Here in this place, enveloped in ancient architecture, steeped in history,
Whilst in contrast, close by,
On the other side of the river,
The future beckons and will not be ignored.
The towering, contemporary skyline speaks of the new, the yet to be explored.

She spoke today of pain and grief,

Reflecting on the place called school.

Expressed how she had never known relief,

Quite like she'd felt when I'd arrived to rescue her,

From their clutches.

The place that had crushed her,

Worn her down.

Denied who she was

Or could be.

She said I'd been her strength when she had nothing left.

Bereft

And lost,

Couldn't see.

But her strength was never truly gone,

Though buried, for so long

She'd needed time to heal,

To explore and to recover,

Discover

Herself

Anew.

Ferocity,

Tenacity,

And a passion for her books.

It

Took

Time.

But today she had arrived
She stood in this ancient place
Years of stories,
Battles,
Loves and loss,
Wrapped her in their power,
History colliding with the yet to come,

In the next minute,
In the next hour…
Time no longer her enemy
Her future hers to own,
To write.

The strength of her convictions had returned,
Shone from within,
Today.

As she turned,

Gave a grin

And began to walk away.

Afterward

So there we are.
Our journey so far.

I truly hope that these words will have touched you in some way. I hope they change some perspectives, and open some eyes; that someone, somewhere, feels a little less along, a little less lost, for having read them.
I wish for our triumphs to bring comfort and hope to those still treading water within the system, fighting for support and recognition.
For the young people and families asking for understanding and compassion.

Because there's such a long way to go.

Only a few days ago, I heard of another beautiful, creative and gentle Autistic young woman who has become so exhausted with the pressure and futility of constant masking, she had taken the step to unalive herself.

And the world continued to turn.

Because you see, people don't like to talk about unsavoury subjects like depression or despair. Or what it means to be neurodivergent in a society where being neurotypical is considered the norm to which we should all aspire.

So I hope that by sharing our truth, and not shying away from the dark and difficult times, together we can celebrate the successes with even more fervour.

This book bears testimony to the grit, determination and chaotic beauty of my children, and their neurokin.

And if you take one thing from our story, let it be this…

Things can change, with the right support and the shared wisdom of those who have walked this path before us.

Hold on.

Keep those who support you and champion your raw authenticity near, seek them out; they are your tribe.

Hold on.

Things can change.
Xx

Acknowledgements

My dearest Brave, beautiful Bumble,
Crazy-funny-lovely Green Bean
And my other half, still makes me laugh, Hubby.
A chapter in our story, and so much more to come.
Love you all

With grateful thanks for your input and support to:

Siobhan Adams	Parenting Mental Health,
Heidi Mavir	Suzanne Anderson
Louise Richards	Polly and Beloved Indie
Sophie Millhench	Ryan, Charlotte and WC clan
Isabelle Rees	Alex Donovan
Emma Bliss	Patch Hyde
Nicky Reid	Deborah and Dave
Kate Hood	Michael Paton
Janice	Mike Marshall
Rachel	Francisco
Sarah	Andy Smith
Cathy	Bex
Mary	Spectrum Gaming
Nala Gunstone	PDA Parenting
Safina Roberts	Steph's Two Girls
Dr Ursual Bax	Dannii
Dr Francesca Tagliente	Benjamin Fudge
	A J O Neil

Natalie Hickman	Deborah Sewell
Emma Foinette	Caspa
Liz	Liz Gale
Jan, Michelle and Ray	Jack Gale
Chloe	The wonderful staff at
Emily	Bromley Bodyshop for going
ADO and River Valley	above and beyond

And last but by no means least, my dearest Martha and Alfie x x

About the Author

Charlotte, a self-identifying Neurodivergent mother of two Neurodivergent teens, brings years of experience both personally, on her own parenting journey, and professionally - as a SEN Teaching Assistant and Emotional Literacy Support Assistant - to her writing.

This anthology of poetry is her first full volume, but she has previously published work in the Sunday Times Bestselling Book "Your child is not broken" by Heidi Mavir, on the Neuroclastic website and within forums online to support other families.

Printed in Great Britain
by Amazon